THE MUSLIMS OF MANIPUR

THE MUSLIMS OF MANIPUR

Salam Irene

KALPAZ

The Muslims of Manipur

Rs. 750

ISBN: 978-81-7835-828-4

Published in 2010 in India by
Kalpaz Publications
C-30, Satyawati Nagar,
Delhi-110052
E-mail: kalpaz@hotmail.com
Phone : 9212729499

Lasser Type Setting by: Rudra Computer Graphics, Delhi
Printed at : Chawla Offset Press, Delhi

Dedication To

For My Husband Rajive and Daughters
Michelle, Andrea and Venetia

Contents

Preface

When one undertakes a study of the Muslims in Manipur, it is immediately apparent that there is a dearth of literature on the subject. It may perhaps be due to the fact that although the Muslims came to Manipur in 1606 AD. they numbered only about a thousand and their number grew only up to 37,197 in 1951. Moreover they were not interested in education till very recently. As a result, there is no authoritative account of the Muslims in Manipur.

This book is an attempt to chronicle the history and culture of the Muslims in Manipur. Their history is unique because not only did they enter the erstwhile kingdom of Manipur as prisoners of war but in a short span of time, they made themselves an integral, indispensable part of Manipur society. They married Meitei women, they adopted Meiteilon as their mother tongue, they attired themselves in Manipuri dress, adopted many features and traditions of the Manipuris, and so came to be named after the dominant community of the Manipur valley and were known as 'Meitei Pangals'. Their leader Muhammad Sani was favored by

King Khagemba and occupied a privileged position in the administration and governance of the kingdom (in the 17th century). Nearly 4 centuries later the first Chief Minister of Manipur State was a Muslim Mhd. Alimuddin. These facts only underline the fact that Muslims won acceptance in Manipur society from the time of their advent into the Kingdom and in every ministry formed after Manipur achieved Statehood in 1972, a Muslim legislator has been a part of the Ministry formation. Relations between the dominant Meitei Hindu majority and the Muslims has been cordial and except for one brief interlude in 1993 amity and harmony has coexisted between the two communities. All these facts only serve to underline the necessity of undertaking, a study of the Muslims in Manipur.

I would like to express my gratitude to my research scholar Ching Simte for the invaluable assistance rendered in typing the manuscript.

Salam Irene

Introduction

Contemporary North East India is a product of British imperialism and Early National Formation of modern India. It is necessary to know how the British empire of the nineteenth century impacted upon the subject people of the North East. The historical experiences of the indigenous peoples therefcre, are attempts to respond to two major influences in history : (i) the structural transformation in society and polity in the wake of imperialism and colonialism, and (ii) the response to the relationship in the context of the modern Indian State.[1]

Manipur is landlocked State located in the eastern most part of the country, sharing an international border with Myanmar. The Indo-Myanmar border is porous and Manipuris can travel by land to Mandalay without a passport. The centrally located amphitheatre like Imphal valley with 700 square mile area is predominantly inhabited by the Hindu and Muslim Meitei communities, totaling 16,74,821 population, and the entire hill areas of 7000 square miles that surround the former, are the abodes of highly heterogeneous 33 tribal ethnic groups with a population of 7,13,813[2]. This geographic division is a determinant factor in the socio-political, historical development of the land.[3]

Manipur was an ancient Kingdom, a cradle of human civilization and creativity, which has come under the influence of many cultures of different ethnic groups who came at various times, and contributed to the growth of the civilization of Manipur. Manipur, being a gateway of India to South East Asia, was influenced by her geographic situation and Ecology in the shaping of her history and cultural development.

Manipur literally means the land of gems. According to Sanamahi Laikan (Manipuri historical work) the name of Manipur was first officially introduced in the early eighteenth century during the reign of Hinduised Garibaniwaza (1709-1748). In the legendary or proto-historical period, the principality which centred at Kangla, the capital of the later Meitei kingdom was known by several names.

Various ethnic groups belonging to southern Mongoloid group - the Tibeto- Burmans, the Indo-Aryans and a sizeable section of Tai (Shans) came to Manipur from pre-historic times down to the present day. The present ethnic groups of Manipur viz., the Meiteis, the Naga tribes, the Kuki - chin tribes and other Indian communities are the descendants of the migrating people (3). (Nongchup Haram' is the term used for those groups of people who came to Manipur from Tripura, Sylhet, Cachar, Assam and adjoining areas as war captives, part of the dowry of a princess (Chingurembi) who married a Meitei Prince, (Kwakpa Thawanthaba) as learned persons employed by the King's court. Muslims came in King Khagemba's reign (1596- 1652), and continued up to King Gambhir Singh's reign (1826-1834). They were known as Meitei Pangal (Pangal - A corrupt form of Bengal) and married local Meitei women, and were assigned sageis (clans). Brahmins came from different parts of India from King Kiyamba's reign (1467-1508) up to King Charairongba's reign. They were assigned 'Yumnaks' (subclans). The chakpas of Manipur were supposedly not original inhabitants but migrated from yunam.[4]

One of the theories of Meitei origin is Aryan, this Aryan connection was an outcome of the adoption of Hinduism by the royal family and the valley people in the eighteenth century, and resultant claim of the descent of the ruling dynasty, from Babhruva Hana, a scion of the Pandava hero, Arjun of the Mahabharata. The fact is that they are neither of the Aryan stock or Indo-Aryan, although they absorbed some Aryan elements from Aryan colonizers, adventurers and immigrants. The representatives of Aryan element are Manipuri Brahmins and the Nongchup Haram. Another theory is the Moi-Tai origin of the Meiteis. All archaeological a'nd historical evidences point to the relationship of ancient Meiteis with the Mon Khmer and Tai people but not of Mon Khmer Tai origin of the people, G. A. Grierson in Linguistic Survey of India' has grouped the Meitei in the Kuki - Chin sub-family of Tibeto - Burman languages. He is generally right in presuming that the ancestors of the Meiteis were among the Tibeto - Burman speakers in S. W. China, Eastern

Tibet and upper Burma. Ch. Budhi Singh asserted, that Meitei or Timei, is an outcome of the ethnic blending of the people of Mei and Ti Tribes of ancient China. Before the coming of the Tibeto - Burman speaking proto - Meitei tribesl, there were Mon - Khmer speaking austroloid mongoloid people, later absorbed by the Tibeto- Burmans. Indo-Aryans and Tais were also absorbed. Ethnologically and linguistically, the Meiteis are Tibeto - Burman of the Southern Mongoloid with Austroloid, Aryan and Tai admixtures.

It. is not dear how the name 'Naga' originated. It is an old name, popularized by the Ahoms and British. The latter gave the generic name to the present Nagas of Nagaland, Assam and Manipur. In Manipur, people were known by their tribe name. Naga legends tell of their migration and settlement in Manipur. It is reliably believed that these tribes were in occupation of the present habitat in the early centuries of the Christian era, or even before that. Naga tribes of Manipur are Tangkhul, Zemi, Liangmei, Rongmei (Zeliangrong) including Puimei, Mao, Maram, Maring, Anal, Moyon, Monsang, Lamgang, Chothe, Thangal, Koireng, Chiru, who are all Tibeto - Burman speakers.

Some Kuki tribes migrated to the Manipuri hills in pre-historic times but greater migration occurred in the eighteenth century. The Kuki - Chin tribes are Thadou, Paite, Hmar, Vaiphei, Gangte, Simte, Zou, Biate, Mizo.[5]

The Muslims of Manipur

The court chronicle of the Kings of Manipur, the 'Cheitharon Kumpapa, refers to the invasion of Manipur by a combined force of Kachari and Muslim mercenaries in 1606 AD. The King of Manipur at the time took 1000 Pangans (Muslims) into captivity. Together with their leader, these Muslims were given a place to settle at Moirangkhom Yaiskul. The first migration was followed by others up to the reign of Chandrakirti (1850- 1886). The liberal Manipuri Kings and the hospitable Manipuri society nurtured the growth of this small community which never felt insecure in Manipur. The population of the Pangals increased gradually. . In the most recent census (2001), the Muslim population was recorded as 1,90,939 constituting 8.32% of the total state population of Manipur.

In family life and social organisation, the Muslim migrants were greatly influenced by Meitei family institutions and social organisations. They imbibed, assimilated and made their own, many of these traditions. Kinship is the basis of the social structure and the Muslims were grouped into 'sageis', where there are about fifty Muslim clans in Manipur. Members were related by blood and the 'most conspicuous events of domestic life centred around the various stages of growth in the life of a person. Stratification in society was based upon occupation - Muslims in the King's army were known as 'Khunja' and those who pursued peaceful vocations were known as 'Ingkhol'.

The vast majority of the Manipuri Muslim resides in villages but 92.9% possess or own land. Availability of water initially decided their choice of habitat. The household size of Manipuri Muslims is 6.3 and there is a strong preference for boys. Muslims by large subsist on the age old agro-oriented pursuits; primarily agriculture (80%). Prior to the advent of colonial rule, the Muslims were liable to render 'Iallup' (compulsory feudal service) to the state. Seventy per cent of Muslims are fish farmers; they also favor poultry-farming. They are a number of skilled artisans in the Muslim community. Most Muslim women work in the unorganized sector - they invest little and earn a pittance, their earnings are not consumerate with the labour and time spent in working.

Like the Turks of Central Asia who established an empire in India in the thirteenth century and the Mughals who followed them in the sixteenth century and who made India their home, the Muslim who came to Manipur from 1606 onwards made Manipur their home. In the process of their settlement, they adopted and assimilated much of Manipur's culture, the degree of assimilation and inculturation was extremely high. But what distinguished these Muslims was their profession of the Islamic faith. One of the most significant contributions of the Jamait in Manipur was the establishment of a chain of madrassas.

From among the Muslims who came to Manipur in 1606 AD, the King appointed Muhammed Shahni as one of the 'Pongba Tara' (Ten ministers). He was the first Muslim to be so appointed. Separate administrative departments were set up for the governance of the Muslims; like the Mangkan Shang and the Pangal Shanglen. Each Muslim Khul (village), had a Muhallah attached to the masjid. A Muslim Panchayat was also constituted in 1891-92 with five Muslim members.

When the Maharaja of Manipur constituted a Manipur State Constitution Making Committee on

12th December 1946 of fourteen members, one member was a Muslim. So also in the Interim Council of 1947, Maulvi Bashiruddin Ahmed was made a Minister. According to the Manipur State Constitution Act of 1947; the State assembly reserved three seats for Muslims. In the election to the State assembly in 1948, five Meitei Pangals were elected. And when Manipur attained Statehood' Muhammed Alimuddin was elected as the first Chief Minister. Ever since a Muslim has always held one or more cabinet rank since 1972. Muslim women however played no direct role in administration, governance and politics till very recently although they have participated in the Nupi Lan of 1939 (Women's War) and in mass movements such as those to preserve the territorial integrity of Manipur and to prevent human rights violations.

However because of their late state in education, the Muslims are largely today a backward community and special programmes need to put in place to ensure them of a rightful position in society.

References

1. Lokendra Arambam – Ethnicity and Politics of Identity – The Manipur experience, 2005.

2. T.S. Gangte – Land problems and ethnic tension in North East India with special reference to Manipur, 2005.

3. Gangmumei Kabui – History of Manipur, Vol. 1, Pre-colonial period, p. 8.

4. N. Debendra Singh – Identities of the migrated people in Manipur.

5. Manorama Sharma – History and History writings in North-East India, pp. 78-80.

1

The Coming of The Muslims To Manipur

Unlike in Indian history, there is no clear-cut division of Manipur's history into the three traditional nomenclatures of Ancient, Medieval and Modern History. There is no clearly acknowledged starting point for the history of medieval Manipur. In Indian History, the medieval period covers the period of rule of the Delhi Sultanate and the Mughal Empire. But in Manipur, the Muslims came not as conquerors, to rule the kingdom, nor as traders, or preachers, but as prisoners of war, in the year 1606 A.D. They came from Bengal. But in what circumstances, did Bengal come under Muslim influence?

Sometime in 1243-44, Residents of Lakhnauti, a city in North-Western Bengal, told a visiting historian, of the dramatic Events that had taken place there, forty years earlier. A band of several hundred Turkish cavalry had ridden swiftly down the Gangetic plain in the direction of the Bengal Delta. Led by a daring officer, Mohammed Bakhtiyar, and disguising themselves as horse-dealers, Bakhtiyar and his men, slipped into the Royal city of Nudiya. They rode straight to the king's palace. Utterly overwhelmed, for he had just sat down to dine, the Hindu Monarch hastily departed, abandoning his capital altogether. This coup d'etat inaugurated an Era, lasting over five centuries, during which most of Bengal was dominated by rulers professing the Islamic faith .[1]

Bengal's historical experience was extra-ordinary, not only in its widespread reception of Islam, but also in its frontier character. In part, the thirteenth century Turkish drive Eastward- both to Bengal, and within Bengal, was the end product of a process triggered by political convulsions in thirteenth century inner Asia. For several centuries, before and after the Mongol irruption into West Asia, newly Islamicised turks from Central Asia, and the Iranian plateau, provided a ready supply of soldiers for commanders such as Mohammed Bhakhtiyar .Once within Bengal's fertile delta, these men pushed on until stopped only by geographical barriers. Surrounded on the north and East by Mountains and to the South by the Sea, Bengal was the terminus of a continent wide process of Turko-Mongol conquest and migration. It was in short, a frontier Zone.[2]

With reference to Manipur, the Mussalman population of Manipur 'has undoubtedly arisen almost entirely from immigrant Bengalis, chiefly from the districts of Silhet and Cachar, who have formed connection with the women of the country, and settled in the valley. All the Mussalman have a decidedly Bengali cast of countenance [3] E.W. Dun stated too, that 'the Mussalmans are the descendants of Bengali Immigrants; they retained knowledge of Hindusthani and Bengali, and hardly distinguishable in appearance from the Bengalis, who had never left Cachar.[4] Henry Yule stated that Kathe Mussalmans (Early Manipuri Muslims) were descendants from inter mixing of Muslims coming in different Eras from different directions-Arakan, Cachar and Manipur itself. Silk spinning was a trade widely followed by Kathe Muhammadans of Arakan,Manipur and perhaps Cachar.[5] B.C. Allen opined that Manipuri Muslims are the descendants of migrants from Surma valley,who came in waves in different periods and married Meitei women in Manipur.[6]

By the time, Mohammad Bhakhtiyar conquered North West Bengal in 1204; Islamic political thought had already evolved a good deal from its earlier vision of a centralized, universal Arab Caliphate. Between the ninth and eleventh centuries, there was a movement of clans, tribes, and whole confederations of Turkish-speaking people from Inner Asia to the Caliphate's Eastern provinces. Coming as military slave soldiers, as migrating pastoral nomads, or as armed invaders, these Turks settled in Khurasan. As Baghdad's Central Authority slackened, Turkish military might, provided the military basis for new dynasties, some Iranian, some Turkish.[7]

The Raja Ganesh period (1411-1414) was a turning point in Bengal history. Bengali Hindus were formally integrated into the Sultanate's ruling structure. Similarly, in 1606, the Muslim soldiers captured by King Khagemba of Manipur, were allowed to enjoy equal status with the Meiteis, and given many opportunities[8]. Not having brought wives and families with them, they were given Meitei ladies to marry, and gradually became integrated with local society.

According to R. Brown, the Muhammadans of Manipur married Manipuri women. Their ranks were further swelled by marriage between the female descendants of these people and Manipuris. Muslims have a native name 'Meitei Pangal', indicating their mixed heritage; they are indigenized and Manipurised like other ethnic groups[9]. The line separating Pangals from Meiteis was porous, tenuous and shifting. The first children of mixed marriage were neither product of Hindu or Muslim culture, but a single Manipuri culture.

The word 'Pangal' is derived from the word 'Bangal'-meaning men of East Bengal. The earliest Muslim settlers came from East Bengal and were consequently called the 'Bangals', meaning the Bengalees of East Bengal. The word 'Bangal' soon corrupted into 'Pangal', because most Manipuris in the seventeenth century pronounced 'b' as 'p'. In Medieval times, any man from East Bengal, irrespective of his religion, was called 'Pangal'. There are Pathans and Moghuls among the Manipuri Muslims[10]. The Mughals had ruled Bengal from the mid- sixteenth to mid-eighteenth century (1567-1765), and Sylhet from 1612, till the colonial advent.

An Inscription from Sylhet town dated 1512-13 mentions that a certain Sikandar khan Ghazi conquered the town (1303-4). Shah Jalal reached Sirhat (Sylhet), one of the areas of the province of Bengal with 313 persons. The famous Moroccan traveler Ibn Batuta (d.1377) personally met Shah Jalal in 1345. He wrote:' This Shaikh was one of the great saints. The inhabitants of these mountains had embraced Islam at his Hands.' It is thus possible that in Shah Jalal, these hill people had their first intense exposure to a formal, literate, religious tradition. The Muslims in Bengal were divided into ashraf and non- ashraf. These groups constituted the earliest known class of Bengali Muslims[12]. The fourteenth century marked the beginning of Islamic influence in Sylhet.

Four conventional theories of Islamization in India have been put forward by Eaton, but none of them are entirely applicable to Manipur, which up to 1891 was an independent, erstwhile kingdom. The immigration theory, views Islamization in terms of the diffusion, not of belief, but of peoples. But according to the most recent census of 2001, the Muslims population constitutes only 8.32% of the total state population of Manipur i.e. 1,90,939 persons.[13] The oldest theory of Islamization in India- Religion of the sword thesis, stresses the role of military force in the diffusion of Islam in India, and elsewhere. But Manipur was never conquered by the Muslims. A third theory commonly advanced to explain Islamization in India, is the religion of Patronage theory. (To receive some non-Religious favor from the ruling class). In Manipur, as the Muslims were never rulers, the question of according non-religious favour never arose. On the other hand, right from the advent of muslims into the kingdom, the Kings of Manipur, gave the immigrant Muslims, local ladies to marry, land to settle in, as also yumnaks (clans). W. Ibohal writes: "The Muslim community of the Meiteis, were also allotted family title or yumnak Sagei, According to their occupation: The Muslims of Manipur, never had an assumed desire for social improvement or prestige. A fourth theory, Religion of Social Liberation thesis, postulates a Hindu Caste system that is unchanging through time, and rigidly discriminating against its own lower order. But when Islam arrived in Manipur, there was no caste system prevalent in the kingdom-the Meiteis had not yet embraced Hinduism. Wise offered a number of arguments to explain how and why, ethnic Bengalis became Muslims. He invoked the Religion of the sword thesis-'enthusiastic soldiers penetrating the dense forests of the Eastern frontier, planted the crescent in the villages of Silhet'. He also propounded the social liberation thesis. But Khondkar Fuzli Rubbee in "The Origin of the Mussalmans of Bengal' states:' 'the ancestor of the present Mussalmans of this country were certainly those Muslims who came here from foreign parts, during the rule of the former sovereign.' He also cited numerous charitable grants (AIMA) to venerable Muslims in Bengal, suggesting that these became the basis of foreign settlement. In the decade before 1947, three Anthropological studies agreed that the masses of Bengali Muslims were descended from indigenous communities. Finally in 1960, D.N. Majumdar and C R Rao published a study: 'We should look among the tribal and scheduled caste non-Muslim groups of Bengal for a possible origin of the muslim population in Bengal.'[15]

In the late sixteenth century, a dynasty of Chaghatai Turks, commonly known as the Mughals, annexed Bengal to their vast empire ; Bengal was now administered by a class of imperial officers who regularly rotated through the realm, sharing a larger pan-Indian view of their political mission.' With Islam Khan's arrival, the Mughal Era of Bengal history effectively began (1610-1704). The Mughal succeeded in annihilating or winning over, all the major chiefs entrenched in the country side since the time of the Sultans. By the mid-seventeenth century; the Mughals had established both power and credibility through the delta[16]. But in the Northern Frontier, there was resistance to imperial authority. To the north, following the Brahmaputra river upstream, Mughal officers encountered peoples who responded very differently to the imposition of imperial rule. In their efforts to dominate this region, the Mughals followed the footsteps of earlier muslim governors and sultans, who had made repeated invasions of the region, with results ranging from temporary success to utter catastrophe. By July 1613, both Kuch Bihar (Cooch Behar) and Kamrup had been annexed, and brought under Mughal Fiscal administration. Around August-September 1615, they launched a full scale invasion of Assam.[17]

The ultimate Islamization of Bengal delta begins with the period of Sultan Shams-Al-din Iliyas Shah's founding of Bengal's first independent Muslim dynasty, and closed with the death of Isa Khan. Cut off from North India, and deprived of fresh military or administrative recruits from points west, Bengal's rulers in this period found their political moorings in local society and culture. The delta was drawn into an Indian Ocean commercial network, permeated by an Islamic ethos.

This was a world system in the wider sense of an arena for the circulation of shared texts and values, sustained by Sufis, pilgrims, merchants, adventurers, scholars and soldiers. Both the nature of that system, and Bengal's inclusion in it, are seen in Ibn Batuta's 1345 visit to Sylhet.[18]

This then is the background of the Muslims who came to Manipur in 1606-Khangemba Khunthok. The court chronicle of the kings of Manipur, the 'Cheitharon Kumpapa and a text known as' Nongshamei Puya', refer to the invasion of Manipur by a combined force of Kachari and Muslim mercenaries. But there is a stay reference made in the Ningthourol Lambuba, about a group of invaders known as the Thongnang who came from the south western side led by one Hasom and Naran. They were Bodo-Kacharis from Tripura or Kachari kingdom, who invaded South-West Manipur. Hasom might have been a corruption of Hasan, a Muslim adventurer. Khagemba (1597-1652) who was the most illustrious ruler of medieval Manipur tried during his reign of fifty years to check the Muslim invasion from the west and defended the kingdom of Manipur from several foreign invaders like the Muslim, Kachari and the Shans of kabaw valley.[19]

The Kachari-Muslim invasion of 1606 was an outcome of an unhappy trifling incident at the Royal palace of Manipur. King Khagemba had two brothers, Chingsomba and Sanongba. There was a boat race in which his brother Chingsomba borrowed the boat of Sanongba, which was broken due to a collision during the boat race. Sanongba wanted the original boat in the condition in which he had loaned it. The issue came to be known as "Shanongba Higaiwa". Khagemba intervened in favor of Kwairakpa Chingsomba. Sanongba took exception to it and fled to Cachar along with his mother Queen Dowager Luwang Changbambi and other nobles. He approached the Kachari king, who was his brother-in- law, to invade Manipur, and restore him to the throne of Manipur. The Cachari king (named as Sapradas Narayan) accepted the request, and sent his general, Takharek and Bhimbal who was his brother with a Kachari Force in 1604 A.D. The Meitei forces were defeated and retreated towards the capital. Khagemba summoned all the nobles and appealed to them to repulse the Kachari forces. According to the Puya, some brave Meitei nobles took the leaders of the invaders as prisoners. Yakharek surrendered to Khagemba, however, the retreating Kachari soldiers informed their king that Yakharek, Bhimbal, and Sanongba betrayed them, and became allies of the king of Manipur.[20] A. Rahman citing Musalman'-e-Manipuri, written in Urdu by Maulana Rahim –uddin, mentions three Muslims, viz, Shaik Ruba, Gora Khan and Ashique Shah who came to Manipur from Rajbari (Pratapgarh Rajabari) and settled in Manipur with Royal permission. Pala Koireng was one Pangal among the Manipuri soldiers in the attack on the Kacharis.[21]

The Kacharis King now engaged one Praseng a leader of the Muslim mercenaries of a locality known as Taraf somewhere near Habigunj in Eastern Bengal. The king deputed another invading force under the command of Yakharek, Bhimbal and Prasena. This was a joint Kachari and Muslim invasion of Manipur in 1606 A.D.[22] The King of Cachar had requested the king of

Taraph, Mohammad Najira, to extend his co-operation in waging war against King Khagemba of Manipur. The Muslim troops crossed to the plains through Khoupom, and established a camp on the banks of Sarel Yangoi. The Cachari troops remained on the upper hills of Khoupom observing the situation. According to R.K. Sanahal Singh, King Khagemba collected many brave people, and constructed a Fortress on the southern side of the Sharai to Haoyen Yangoibaung.[23] The Royal chronicles records the invasion by the Mayangs (Kachari) and Sanongba. Nawab Najira sent a Muslim contingent consisting of 1007 soldiers under the generalship of his younger brother Mohammad Shahni (Bor), who was accompanied by sixteen leaders, viz. Munon khan, Aman, Monai, Akon, Aluf, Chuleiya, Namfa, Faitong, Tumiya, Qamaya, Khendo, Aqya, Sapra Muhmad, Punot, Ayamba and Kashra.[24]

The Army was divided into two sections-the Muslim troops were placed under the command of General Shahni, and the Cachari troops under Yakharek and Bhimbal. The overall commander of the combined troops was Sanongba. King Khagemba constructed a fortress, divided it into four parts, and each side was defended by a group of troops. The King prepared a contingent of 180 cavalry and two guns[25]. He was assisted by his younger brother Chingsomba and General Nongshamei of the Lairikyengbam. The invading forces were defeated. Sanongba was captured, and a large number of invading forces, including their leaders were taken prisoners.[26]

When the Cachari troops were retreating, the Kabuis of Khoupum informed the Manipuri troops of the retreat. A battle ensued; Khagemba fell down from his horse. When he was on the ground, a Muslim soldier Munon khan tried to kill him, but he was saved by Nongsamei (Dhananjoy), who attacked Munom Khan with a spear. The Cachari troops fled without informing Mohammad Shani. Now only the Muslim troops remained. As their military strength was considerable, and greater than that of the troops of Khagemba, the Manipuri king decided to have recourse to diplomatic measures as a means of diffusing the situation. He sent Nongsamei, who was well-versed in different languages like Parshi, Cachari and Bengali, to negotiate terms with the Muslims leaders, to withdraw their respective troops. However after the agreement had been arrived at, the Manipuri soldiers surrounded the Muslim troops who were unarmed, And made an offer of surrender or death.[27] The Muslims wisely chose the first option. The Cheirtharon Kumpapa states that Khagemba "captured thirty elephants, one thousand guns, and a colony of 1000 Pangans, including swordsmiths, brass smiths, and other skilled men, makers of trumpets and long drums, those who could make bracelets, Washermen, Horse grooms, grooms for elephants, all these were captured. All those Pangans who were captured alive were allowed to establish an institute.[28] However, according to Gangmumei Kabui, this is a hyperbolic account. The kachari- Muslim invasion failed and most of the soldiers were not professional soldiers but common peasants who were promised rich rewards, for an adventure in an unknown land.[29]

In the Royal chronicle, the term 'pangan' is used first in 1556 (sakabda 1478)- "the year of Thingpaicham Pangan, and in1557 –" The year of Pangaracha Khara,

Sakabda 1479. Also the chronicle Sakabda 1529 (1607CE) mentions the year of Thingkurum Pangan (A Muslim with Meitei surname.[30]

The impact of the invasion (1606) on Manipur was quite profound. The influence of the Muslim civilization under the imperial Mughals was felt in Manipur. The Muslim prisoners were settled and they constituted a useful community in the kingdom.[31]

The 'Khagemba Lanpha', a Royal chronicle recorded the names of some of the Muslim prisoners. Nongsamei captured Heiyaimot (Hayat Muhammad) a phusaba (potter), Shuqton (Shuqar-uddin), a khut-heiba, skilled in red sugar mill (kollu), A Mangkhan weaver and sepoy. Thiyam Pungshon captured Ulamot (Ulf Muhammad) a phundrei (turner) Satpam Saraba captured Alimsha (Alim Shah) who was allowed to settle in Yairipok. The last also captured Ali (Phundrei) And Shekh (Shaikh) a black smith. Who were allowed to settle in Noongchai and Solai. Two brothers, Mewarmot (Manawar Muhammad) and Kosarmot (Kausr Muhammad) as also Tona of Mursidabad were captured. Other immigrant Muslims included Tonba from Makak, Leimushek (Rahim-uddin Shaikh) a khut-heiba, and his brothers, Yangba and Manik (Malik), Kharamot from Mughal, Batse (Basir) and his brother Mansara, Yangba, brother of phundrei Ali, Khamba, brother of Leimusek khut-heiba, Mocha, brother of Shangom Sumbam Ngangba from Mobur. Ngangba who came from Mursidabad, brother of Tona and Malik, was appointed Qazi by the King of Manipur. The Last Captives among the mercenary Taraf soldiers in 1606 were Khamba, brother of Cheinandi (Zeinab Bibi) and Kasr Muhammad.[32]

After 1606, many more Muslims came to Manipur and settled. The Muslims who had migrated to Manipur after1606 were mostly soldiers. After settling in Manipur, they had been given local surnames, and took part in a number of wars. They became an indispensable part of Meitei society, The Muslims were given Manipuri ladies to wed and settled in Manipur permanently.[33] Thus, the pluralistic foundation of Manipur's society was further strengthened. The Muslims were given several economic occupations. The liberal, social policy of Manipur allowed the Muslims to follow their religion and particular way of life. A department was created under a Kazi, who would administer Muslim personal law for the immigrants.[34] The Muslims adopted Islam in a strict manner only after 1910 A.D. Prior to 1910 A.D. there was no hard and fast rule with regard to religion and faith. The Muslims being hard workers excelled in many disciplines. They were also provided many opportunities, as also equal status with the Meitei.[35]

Although the actual settlement of the Muslims in Manipur commenced from 1606 A.D., there are references to Muslim entry into Manipur, prior to this date. According to the Puyas, Lairen Nawphangba (594-624A.D.) invited a Pangal Muslim guru (saint) who recently came to Manipur from the West, to Kangla, to help build the Kangla Throne.[36] Sakok Lamlen Ahanba and Kangla Houba Pakhangba also refer to this event. John Parrat observed that the first

Muhammadans, the Aribam family, came to Manipur in the time of Naophangba.[37] N. Devendra and the Muslim Panchayat Lilong Report (1932) noted that two persons, Sadir Para Koireng and Kutuwan Khan, were the progenitors of the Pangal Aribam clan. The London School of Oriental and African studies, made available a document in 1983, which made possible studies on the process of the formation of the various clans, about fifty in number. The document noted that the Palace Pandits (Meitei scholars) are of the view that Manipuri Muslim clan formation, initiated with what is named as 'the Aribam Sagei' since the period of king Naophangba (590-680 A.D.). This Pangal population as found in 930 AD was adept in preparing Salt from dug wells, since their Muslim co-religionists used to collect salt from the Bengal Sea, According to B. Kulachandra Sharma (1997:62)[38] Sanskrit, Vaishnavite and Meitei Puya sources, referred to the Seventh to the fourteenth century Muslims as 'Turushka'.[39] Royal chronicle 'Ningthourel Lambuba' described two Pasha and one Pangal village that flourished during the reign of King Irengba (984-1074 A.D.) Living at Khuga valley at that time, these Pangals introduced the practice of 'Rice broadcast and transplantation' procedure in Manipur.[40] Prior to the seventeenth century; Muslims were divided into four groups Viz. Shaikh, Syed, Pathan, Mughal.[41] The group was numerous enough to form a clan, and king Naophangba conferred on them the clan name 'Aribam'.

It is said that during the reign of king Mungyamba, three Muslims named Seikh Ruba, Gora khan and Ashiq Shah came to Manipur from Rajabari (probably

Khaspur). They could manufacture muskets, and the king ordered them to manufacture the same. These three Muslims married Manipuri women. And they were the Forefathers of the Manipuri Muslim clan known as 'Aribam Sagei' (oldest clan).[42]

The earliest reference however to 'Pangal' According to W. Ibohal Singh, is found in the account that states that Nongyai Thingkonhamba, father-in-law of Irengba, and Khuman chief, went on an assault on the southern Loijing ranges inhabitated by Pangals (Kouba umeiram umei lengkai chingda khousaba pangal Mar khulenleigi kala Raja lamjingba).[43]Another Muslim saint came to Manipur in the reign of King Irengba. Historical reference e.g. (Puya 'Leithak Leikharol) of establishment of Pathan and Pasha Ningthourol in Manipur would indicate Muslim principalities or chieftainship'. There had been Manipuri speaking Ethnic Manipuri Muslims (Pangals) found in eighty villages, towns and inhabitations and having forty-eight clans. They spoke languages – Urdu, Farsi Turki, Arabic etc. before, but they started adopting Meiteilon (Manipuri) by the time of King Khunjaoba (1652-1666 A.D.), but they for long continued to use many words and phrases of these languages.[44]

Edward Gait supported Mc Culloch's view that "The Munniporee Mussalman population arose from Munnipore men having taken as wives Mussalman women.....before the regular introduction of Hinduism. On the introduction of that religion, they with their descendants were obliged to become Mussalmans". This original population was increased by Mussalmans from the West, who came and settled in Munnipore.[45] But

Mirza Fazlul Quadir wrote that Manipur Muslims grew out of the local converts into Islam. Very few Muslims from the rest of India went and settled in Manipur State. The major portion of Manipur's Muslim population is by conversion. Muslims never ruled in that territory. During British Rule, only a few Muslims from other parts of India settled in Manipur state. In Thoubal, Moijing village, there is a clan called 'Monsam', whose Forefathers converted to Islam. Formerly, they belonged to some tribe. The people of Moijing village, sometimes, call the members of this particular clan as hillmen."[46] Hodson was of the view that 'the Panggan or Muhammadan inhabitants of Sylhet and Cachar resemble the hill type. The Panggans are believed to have originated from Cachar as prisoners of war taken by the Meitei's[47] J. Roy stated that "The ancestors of the Muslims families of Manipur came at different times from Sylhet and Cachar. They took Manipuri wives and settled in Manipur.[48] R. Brown wrote that 'the Meithei or Manipuri proper included Mussalmans or Meitei Pangal. Manipuri's said that from great antiquity Mussalmans have formed part of the valley, as well as the Hindus. Muslims have a native name Meitei Pangall, indicating their mixed heritage... (It) indicates the extent of their acculturation, acclimatization and assimilation.[49] The Muslims inhabited the fertile tracts of land on the bank of the Imphal and Iril rivers. Those Muslims, who had accompanied Muhammad Shahni, were given a place to settle at Moirangkhom Yaiskul.

In 1608, three Muslims Viz. Sayid Ambia son of Sayid Auriya, the religious advisor of Taraf king Muhammad Nazeri, Sayid Abdullah, and Shaikh Husain migrated to Manipur. They too were given Meitei wives, and land for settlement. In king Khunjaoba's reign (1652-1666), seven persons from Makak, inclusive of three Muslims viz. Isakrumulla Marumbi Bibi Photma and son Musa Kalamulla came to Manipur. The first was given land at Apong Ingkhol, Imphal. In Paikhomba's Reign (1666-1697), thirty-seven Muslim travelers arrived from Makak led by Milaya Sheikh, Prince of Makak. They Presented valuable gifts of an elephant, palanquin, pearls and sheep to the king of Manipur,[50] and were granted domicile, wives and a livelihood in 1679. Six Muslims from Gujarat too came and received the same privileges. In April 1671, two Shaikh Brothers of Mughal and Konok on Mughal horses arrived at the capital of Manipur. Three Pangals- Chuki Meihaiba, Huipuba and Singga khongba who worked in the Pangal Mall and Singga Loishang of Manipur visited Tripura in 1676 and then returned[51].

The Cheitharon Kumpapa mentions (1701) Saturday, full moon, Nasom Cha Aaroi/ Pukhranpa and others (including a Muslim), tried to put Yipungo Loiyamba on the throne. (The mention of a Meetei Muslim (pangan) amongst the group is indicative, as Muslims are not idolatrous, and hence joined the objection against the king's introduction of idols through the Meetei divinities, the Lais, Despite their peaceful settlement in Manipur, the Royal chronicle mentions (1721) "the Month of Yinga (May/June) began on Monday.14 Sunday as the Kapos, and the Pangans challenged each other. In a battle Haopamcha, the Pukhranpa led the Pangans, and they all went to attack Somsok. 23rd Tuesday, they returned.

The migration of the Muslims to Manipur continued up to the Reign of Chandrakirti (1850-1886). In 1731, it was written: 'the Month of Poinu (November/ December) began on Friday. Haopamcha, the Pukhranpa's child (daughter) was married to Sana Aahan. 17 Saturday, the Pangan Senlungpa, who was the father of Leima, left to receive the beasts from Mayang. (Leimapokpa: Leima, wife of the king, pokpa (verb) to give birth: the father of one of the wives of the king. He is also referred to as a Pangan Selungpa. It is possible that he was a non-Muslim, and held the post of Selungpa over the Muslims. 1748 A.D. was written as the year of Khutlempa Pangan, Sakabda 1670 (Khutlempa Pangan-A Muslim with a Meitei surname)[52] Quazi Hamid Ali states: "we know from the Nongshamai that the Saiyads came to Manipur during the time of Khagemba Maharaja, and one of them, Saiyid Hussain by name, returning to Bengal, brought the Quran to Manipur. Possibly the Saiyads and Pathans from Gujarat, came to Manipur in search of Fortune[53] Muslim traders, artisans and labourers began to enter into Manipur long before the accession of Gharib Niwaz. In 1661, in the Manipuri month of Poinu (December roughly), some Mughals known to the Manipuris as 'Mangals' visited Manipur. When they left is not recorded. In the same month, three men were sent to visit the Mughal Empire. They returned to Manipur after one year and two months. In Sajibu (about April) 1671, two Mughal brick-makers arrived. They were brothers. A horse too arrived from the Mughal Empire in the same month. The horse was afterwards known as 'the Mughal horse'.[54] The arrival of seven Muslim Faqirs from Cachar in April 1795 was the largest Faqir immigration. Kashoudin (Kasim-uddin) was the leader; Pir Baba of the Faqirs[55]. They effected some change in the way of life of the Meitei Pangals, inclining it towards Islamic beliefs.

In "The Background of Assamese Culture", R.M. Nath writes: Gopal Singh ascended the throne of Manipur in 1709 A.D. at the age of twenty, and assumed the surname "Gharib Niwaz", a honorific epithet given to him by the Emperor of Delhi. Whether or not this was the case, through the medium of religion and commerce, Manipur undoubtedly maintained connections with the neighbouring Muslim province, at the time of Gharib Niwaz Hence there can be little doubt that the word "Gharib Niwaz" used by Pamheiba belongs to the Persian vocabulary. J. Roy writes that in Persian "Gharib Niwaz" means 'Kind to the poor'. In the beginning of the eighteenth century, when the major portion of Eastern India was still under Muslim domination, percolation of a Persian word "Gharib Niwaz" into Manipur, through the Hills, and becoming a favorite of her powerful King, is not at all an impossibility. For even today, long after Muslim Rule, the Muslim titles like Diwan, Munshi, Mazumdar, Bahudar etc. are found very common among the aristocrats of the neighbouring states, both Hindu and Muslim alike. In the year 1667, the Eastern boundary of the Mughal Empire under the generalship of Mir Jumla, extended as far as the Darrang district in Assam. Sylhet and part of Cachar district continued to be ruled by Muslim Amirs appointed by the Nawab of Dacca till 1765.[56] And in the Seventeenth and eighteenth centuries, Manipur had good relations with Taraf, Sylhet, Cachar, Tripura, Makak etc.[57]

During the period of the Seven Years Devastation of Manipur by the Burmese-'Chahi Taret Khuntakpa' 1819-1826, many Muslims along with Meiteis were taken as captives to Burma-other Muslims took shelter at Cachar and Sylhet. One Habibullah Moijingmayum of Thoubal- Moijing, the Shanglakpa during Marjit's Reign, was one of the Meitei Pangals who contributed to the growth of Islamic education in Cachar during the seven years devastation.[58] After 1826, only some of the original Muslim settlers returned to Manipur. R. Brown wrote 'the Mussalman population appears before the devastation of the country by the Burmese, to have attained a considerable amount, but as the case with all other sections of the Manipuri community, the greater portion of it was carried into captivity by these ruthless invaders, and the present Mussalmans are the descendants of the few that escaped capture.[59]

Some Muslims from Cachar and Sylhet as also the Meitei Pangals joined as Sepoys the Manipur Levy in 1824. Shaikh Lobah, Shaikh Shubah, ShaikhChybah, Shaikh Prem (Jamai Mia), Shaikh Brow and Shaikh Seba from Cachar and Sylhet were recruited as soldiers in the Manipur Levy at Jattarpur on 30th July 1824, and after 1826 they were allowed to settle in Manipur.[60]

Another migration of twelve Muslims from Cachar occurred in 1846. With the opening of the office of the British Political Agent in 1835 in Manipur, some Pathans with the permission of the government of Manipur lived in Manipur as British India subjects. Most were workers/soldiers of the British, Few were businessmen. When Manipur merged with the Indian Union, some of their descendants remained in Manipur. They were generally known as 'Pathan Kora Parumiya, (Faruk Mia) Choudhury ran a business at Imphal and rendered his services to King Nar Singh. He was rewarded by the king in 1845.[61] In a rare reference to the Muslim subjects of the King, the Royal chronicle records, that on Friday 23rd, Kalen (about May) in Jai Singh's reign (1763), a muslim named Tomba of Mangan Mayum, presented the king with different kinds of the produce of his garden and field. In turn, he was rewarded.[62]

Maharaja Chandra Kirti Singh was deeply interested in religious matters. His Muslim subjects were fairly treated. It was the custom of all subjects, to pay their respects to the Maharaja by bowing down before him. When Chandra Kirti learnt that it was against Islam (kornish and Taslim were practiced in the court of the Delhi Sultans and the Mughal Emperors), he exempted the Muslims from this practice, and remained content with the salutation, 'Salam". He conferred the title 'Nawab 'on the leader of the Muslim community, who were then about 5000 in number[63]. According to Quazi Hamid Ali, one Muslim Prince from Sylhet visited Manipur during Chandra Kirti's Reign.[64] A Muslim Faqir viz. Baba Longar Shah of Cachar arrived in Manipur in 1850.[65]

HABITATION

The Socio-Economic Survey, Meitei Pangal 2004 states that the Meitei Pangal forms an important, indispensable Religious community in Manipur, and inhabits 95 hamlets/villages sub-blocks of towns, with a total population of 2, 02,355, of which 50.39% are males and 49.61% are females. The Meitei Pangal population is centred mainly in Thoubal and Imphal East Districts;

it is less widely diffused in the districts of Imphal West, Bishnupur, Chandel and Churachandpur.[66] The marriage between Muslim migrants and Meitei women resulted in the growth of Muslim inhabitations in different parts of the Imphal valley. The first Muslims were given a place to settle- Janmasthan Thokchom Leikai, Moirangkhom.[67] The early Manipuri Muslim settlers in Manipur easily embraced the Manipuri culture. The Liberal Manipuri Kings, and the hospitable Manipuri society, nurtured the growth of this small community, which never felt insecure in Manipur.[68]

In the early period of settlement, Muslims were given land adjacent to the Royal Palace and employed as soldiers in the Kings Army. Their Migration in King Khagemba's Reign is referred to as 'Khunthok Achouba' or great migration. R.K. Sanahal states that Lilong (A Muslim dominated inhabitation today) and Mayangkhang (in Chandel district) were the first places allotted for Muslim settlement.[69] Although the habitation pattern cannot be traced in complete detail; information on some important Muslim settlements (villages) is available. The main occupation of the Muslims was agriculture. A village could be inhabited by both Meiteis and Muslims, but generally, the latter established themselves in separate localities of the same Valley. The majority of the Muslims settled on River embankments because of the fertility of the soil, the possibility of additional income from rivers (Fish). Road transport was not well-developed, and rivers afforded an easy means of communication.[70]

In 'Khagemba Lanpha' there is a reference to one Satpam Saraba arresting a Pangal Anilsa and banning him to Yairipok. Another Muslim Phundrei Ali was similarly banished to Nungchai and Saikh, a blacksmith to Sora[71]. In this manner, the Muslim habitations became greatly diffused.

In the year 1608 A.D. three Muslims from Taraf came to Manipur-Sayid Ambiya, Sayid Abdullah and Sayid Qalqa Huisen, led by Bor Shena Lanjinglen and accompanied by Muslims Troops, They went to Tekcham at the side of Khonjom to subdue the hill tribes, and later settled there. In 1630 A.D. King Khagemba ordered Ibrahim Miya and others to settle in Thoubal to provide a defence against attacks by the Maring Tribe. Similarly, Shaikh Shali Mullah was sent to Yairipok for purposes of protection. In 1627 A.D Muhmad Abdul Qarim was sent to settle at Nungchai (Nungjai).[72]

Other settlements sprang up for different reasons. For e.g. as tigers roamed near Keirao, and a Muslim provided the king with this information. The tiger was caught and the settlement was named 'Keirao'. In like manner another Muslim inhabitation,' Urup' was named after an immersed jack fruit tree in the Iril river, from which a statue of Shree Shree Govindajee was carved in Bhagya Chandra's Reign. Muslim settlement at Sangai Yumpham commenced around 1754. Habitation of Muslims in Kshetrigao began in 1853-54, during the Reign of Chandrakirti (1850-1886) four villages emerged viz Kshetri Bengoon, Kshetri, Khergao and Keikhu. The Meitei Pangal settled at Cha-ngam-dabi in 1853-54.The First settlers were Sagol Makok (subol), Lal Miya, Piba Subedar and Isuppa. Food was abundantly available here.[73]

In 1824, the King of Langthabal pleased with the agricultural output of the Muslims gave them land for settlement. Subsequently, Maharaj Kyamba allowed them to settle between Canchipur and Singjamei. They presented agricultural Produce to the king, and because the land was extremely fertile, it was named Kiyamgei, Thambi chao was changed to Pangkhong around 1880- the first settlers here were Rahimudin, Tulab of Khutheipham clan, Sarabuddin, Haji Kiyam, Abdul Ali and Rahimudin of Khullakpam clan, and Abdul Ali and Halim of Pusam clan. Islamadabad came into existence about one hundred and fifty years ago; so named, as the jungle there was made fit for inhabitation by a Muslim. Muslims also settled way back at Uchiwa Wangbal named after a rat that jumped out of a felled bamboo tree. Moijing was named after the Moiching Family who lived on the Thoubal River bank. Two other villages of Muslim settlement were Hayellabuk named after the fruit 'Hayel' and Heibong Makhong named after a fig tree. Loumanga was named after five pari fields and Leihaokhong after the beautiful flowers that grew there. Settlement at Komlakhong commenced about a hundred years ago; in 1960 some Meitei-Pangal migrated from Thoubal and settled at Leitanpokpi, near the bank of the Khuga River, where smooth clay (leitan) was procurable. Muslim Nagar was first inhabited by Ibrahim, Hayad Ali, Halim and another from Sora village of Thoubal district in 1956. Upto 1982, the village was known as Pangaltabi, It was renamed Muslim Nagar after consultation with the first Muslim local club viz. Mohammadan Sporting Youth Club and some local educated individuals.[74]

Acquisition of land is regarded as a fundamental duty of every Manipur Muslim. 'The percentage of households possessing homestead land is 100%, irrigated cultivable land is 21%, unirrigated cultivable land 62%.It is interesting to take cognizance of the fact that the entire Manipuri Muslim reside in their own property. However, most Residences are Kutcha constructions, amounting to 620 out of 1000, semi-kutcha dwellings amount to half of kutcha houses, and only 68 out of 1000 are pucca houses.

The population of the Pangals increased gradually. At the time of their first settlement in Manipur they numbered about 1000. In the 1870's; R. Brown calculated that there about 900 families or 4,500 men, women and children. In 1881, Muhammadans numbered 4,881.[75] According to the decennial census 1951-2001, the Muslim population of Manipur in 1951 was 37,197, in 1961-48,588, in 1971- 70, 969, in 1981-99,327, in 1991-1,33,535 and 2001- 1,90,939, constituting 6.44,6.23, 6.62, 6.99,7.27 and 8.32% of the total state population of Manipur. The growth rate from 1961 onwards was higher than the national average. It stood at 134 in 2001, as against 116 for India as a whole. The Sex ratio is 973 per 1000, Female –headed households are only 7.81 as against 92.19 Male-headed households 41.93% of the population falls in the age group of 0 to 14 years, 53.92% in the age group of 15-59 years, and 4.15% in the age group of 60 and above. The dependency Ratio is worked out as 1:08 for Meitei Pangals as against 1.07 for the State in 1991. This means that there are more earners in the Muslim community as compared to other communities in the State.[76]

References

1. Richard M.Eaton –The Rise of Islam and the Bengal Frontier 1204-1760, p. xxi.

2. Ibid., p. xxii.

3. R. Brown- Statistical Account of Manipur, Delhi 1975, p. 15.

4. E.W. Dun- Gazetter of Manipur, New Delhi 1981, p.14.

5 Henry Yule- A narrative of the Mission of the Court of Ava in 1855, p.156.

6. B.C. Allen- Gazetteer of Naga Hills and Manipur, 1905.

7. Richard M. Eaton op.cit., p. 23.

8. Report on Socio-Economic Survey of Meitei-Pangals (Manipuri Muslims) 2004-Directorate of Economics and Statistics and Directorate of Minorities and other Backward Classes, Government of Manipur, Imphal, p. 8.

9. Salam Irene- Manipur Muslim Women, p. iii.

10. Ibid., cit.R.K. Jhaljit Singh –A short history of Manipur pp. 10-13.

11. Richard M. Eaton, op.cit., p.76.

12. Ibid., p. 101.

13. Report on Socio-Economic Survey of Meitei Pangals, op.cit., p. 23.

14. W.Ibohal Singh- History of Manipur, Early Period, Imphal 1986, p. 608.

15. Richard M. Eaton, op.cit., pp.113-126.

16. Ibid., pp.157, 158.

17. Ibid., pp.187, 189, 190.

18. Ibid., p. 306.

19. Gangmumei Kabui- History of Manipur Vol. I- Pre-colonial period, pp. 206, 210.

20. Ibid., p. 214.

21. A. Hakim Shah Khullakpam-The Manipur Governance to the Meitei Pangal 1606-1949, p. 31.

22. Salam Irene- op.cit., p. 2.

23. R.K. Sanahal Singh- Pangal Thorakpa, Imphal 1989, pp. 7-8.

24. Thangjam Subhas Singh-Socio-Economic condition of the Manipuri Muslims in pre-colonial Manipur (Unpublished thesis- Manipur University 2007) p.18, cit. B. Kullachandra Sharma and Badaruddin- Meitei Pangal Hourakpham, Imphal 1991.

25. Ibid., op.cit., p. 20.

26. Gangmumei Kabui-op.cit., p. 214.

27. Thangjam Subhas Singh, op.cit., p. 22.

28. Saroj Nalini Arambam Parratt- The Cheitharon Kumpapa- Original text, translation and notes, p. 67.

29. Gangmumei Kabui, op.cit., p. 215.

30. Saroj Nalini Arambam Parratt, op.cit., p. 68.

31. Gangmumei Kabui op.cit., p. 215.

32. A.Hakim Shah Khullakpam-op.cit., pp. 34-35 cit. I.Amubi, N. Khelchandra,O. Bhogeswor and N. Ibochouba Ed. Shagei Shalairol, Imphal 1994, pp. 44-45.

33. Report on Socio-Economic Survey of Meitei Pangals 2004 op.cit., p. 8.

34. Gangmumei Kabui, op.cit., p. 217.

35. Report on Socio-Economic survey of Meitei Pangals 2004 op.cit., p. 8.

36. Salam Irene – The Advent of the Muslims and Islamic Institutions in Manipur- Seminar Paper, 2008, p.1.

37. John Parrat (ed) notes of the Meitei Beliefs and Customs, Imphal 1998, p. 83.

38. Salam Irene- Manipur Muslim Women, p. 5.

39. Yengkhom Bhagya- Leithak Leikharol Imphal 1956 pp.112-113.

40. Salam Irene- op.cit.p. 5 cit. O. Bhogeswor Singh- Ninthourel Lambuba, Imphal, V ol. 2, 1967.

41. Asim Raj- The Islamic Syncretistic Tradition in Bengal, New Delhi, Sterling 1983, p. 32.

42. A.Rahman- The Meitei Pangal, p. 460.

43. W.Ibohal Singh-op.cit., p. 216.

44. Farooque Ahmed- Multidimensionality of Ethnicity in Manipur-From conceptions to substantivity, with special reference to Muslim Ethno-historical evolution, Seminar Paper 2005 cit. M. Irabot and Ibehal Devi, 1995 Thainagi Manipur Amasung Mayang Thorakpa p.146, L. Ashok Kumar Manipurgi Haraokumeida Manipur Pangal Singna louriba Thoudang, In Arambam Samrendra Manipur Amasung Meitei-Pangal, 1998, p.11.

45. Md. Ahmed Ali Shah- A Brief Historical Study of Religion and society of the Pangals of Manipur- Unpublished M. Phil dissertation Manipur University 1994.

46. Ibid p.13 cit. M.F. Quadir –Muslims of North East India-Souveniur, North East India 15 century Hijri Era celebration, Gauhati,1981, p. 4.

47. T.C. Hodson- The Meitheis-Reprint 1975, p. 4.

48. J. Roy-History of Manipur 1973, p.171.

49. Farooque Ahmed-op.cit., p.10.

50. Thangjam Subhas Singh, op.cit., pp. 23-25.

51. A. Hakim Shah Khullakpam, op.cit., p. 57.

52. Saroj Nalini Arambam Parrat, op.cit, p.139.

53. Quazi Hamid Ali-The Manipuri Muslim, p.12.

54. Salam Irene op.cit., p. 6 cit R.K. Jhaljit Singh- A short History of Manipur pp.123, 131.

55. A. Hakim Shah Khullakpam op.cit., p. 58.

56. J. Roy, op.cit, pp. 34-35.

57. A. Hakim Shah Khullakpam, op.cit, p. 57.

58. Ibid., p. 60.

59. R. Brown, op.cit, p.15.

60. A. Hakim Shah Khullakpam, pp..60-61.

61. Ibid.

62. R.K. Jhaljit –A Short History of Manipur, p. 203.

63. J. Roy op.cit, p. 96 cit. Johnstone- My Experience in Manipur and Naga Hills.

64. Quazi Hamid Ali op.cit., p.15.

65. R.K. Sanahal, op.cit., p. 43.

66. Report on Socio-Economic Survey of Meitei Pangal 2004 p.14.

67. B. Khullachandra and Badruddin-Meitei Pangal Hourakpham, Chingtam Press Naoremthong Bazar Feb.1991, p. 24.

68. Khairuddin Choudhury- The Culture of Manipuri Muslim- a look- Souveniur of Fourth Annual Conference of the All Assam Manipuri Muslim Students Welfare Union, Cachar, Assam.

69. Thangjam Subhas Singh op.cit., p. 32. R.K. Sanahal, Satjal, Imphal 1970, p. 252.

70. Mahmoodah Khaanam- The System of Education prevalent among the Muslims of Manipur-Unpublished dissertation Manipur University 1990, cit. Chander

Sheikhar Panchani- Manipur Religion, Culture and Society, pp. 75,104.

71. Thangjam Subhas Singh- op.cit.p.32 cit. R.K. Sanahal Singh- Manipur Shamajda Muslim (pangal) Shingi Dan, Mingshel, Imphal 1980, p. 8, A. Amubi, N. Khelchandra and O.Bhogeshor (ed) Khagemba Lanpha p. 8, B. Kullachandra Sharma, Meitrabak Khunthok Khundarol, Imphal 1997, p. 92.

72. Op.cit. p. 33 cit. O. Bhogeswor Singh and M.A. Janab Khan; Nongsamei, Imphal 1973 p. 82, B. Kullachandra and Badaruddin op.cit, p. 94.

73. Report on Socio- Economic Survey of Meitei Pangals 2004 op.cit, pp.15-17.

74. Ibid.

75. Md. Ahmad Ali Shah op.cit.p.21 cit. L. Iboongohal p.164, R. Brown p.15, E.W. Dun, p.14.

76. Report on Socio- Economic Survey of Meitei Pangals 2004 op.cit., pp. 23, 25, 27, 28.

2

Social Life

In family life and social organisation, the Muslim migrants into Manipur, were greatly influenced by Meitei family institutions and social organisation. They imbibed, assimilated and made their own, many of the traditions pertaining to family life and organisation of the Meiteis.

Societal relations are defined by the patriarchal concept, where the father is the head of the family. The eldest son of the head of a clan was known as 'Piba' and considered to be the leader of the clan. He worked outside the home, while the women remained busy with domestic chores and weaving. There was no distinction of high and low among the sageis (clans) of the Manipuri Muslims[1]. The society is democratic and has no class distinction[2].

Kinship is the basis of social structure, and a man is identified by the clan to which he belongs. Most families are nuclear, but there are several joint families too. The nuclear family is predominant. Women are also entitled to inherit paternal property[3]. The parents select a suitable son, generally the youngest, to continue to live with them. Inheritance and succession take place through the male line; Sons receive an equal share of the father's property, and the youngest receives the major share.

The kinship system of the Pangals is greatly influenced by the Meitei cultural and social structure. 'Shagei' is a kinship group and members are related by blood[4]. By 'kinship' is meant a social relationship based upon family relatedness, as culturally defined. The culture determines which family relationships are considered significant, what the rights and obligations of specific types of related persons are and what forms of organisation, exist among related persons. Some Anthropologists limit the term 'kinship' to consanguineal relationships i.e. relationships based on ties of blood, but affinal relationships i.e. relationships based on marriage, form an essential part of any kinship system. All types of kinship, primary, secondary, tertiary, affinal and consanguineous, are found in the social system of the Pangals[5]. Despite Quranic sanction, Muslims refrain from marrying within the same 'Shagei'. Such relationship is viewed as taboo, and the King (of Manipur) forbade all such practices and punished violators. After Manipuri's merger with India (1949), instances of such marriage have been recorded, but they are frowned upon.

Shageis can be closely knit or vice versa. A shagei contains many families- 'Yumnaks'of the same clan. These are further sub-divided into Singlup' or Sub clans.

It is possible for two or more Yumnaks to combine to form a Shagei eg. Khulakpam and Shajaobam, as they possessed common forefathers. Similarly, there are also separate entities in a shagei based on factors like profession, physical features, place of residence, e.g. Maibam Angouba and Maibam Amuba, also Harithabam and Awang. In a shagei, there are normally 'Phurups' shinglups, kangbu or khut, groups based on lineage, social and customary considerations. The last is based on the lineage of primary kinship, and members are compact, standing for a specific interest and different and distinct from Phurup and Singlup. Phurup is a group comprising mainly of shagei members. It includes the neighbors in the leikai, and so is not compact, but each member helps the other. A Shinlup is a closely-knit group of the members of a Shagei of a particular area kin-group. On auspicious occasions like marriage or a feast, the members of singlup are bound together in mutual assistance, and feed and house family and relatives coming from distant areas[6].

Every Manipuri Muslim village is like a united body possessing voluntary societies performing different functions. The spirit of mutual help in well and woe, can be explained by a few examples. On the occasion of marriage, every village contributes in cash and kind to the concerned family, besides helping the family in making the marriage arrangements. In the event of death, villagers contribute rice and other cooked food to the bereaved family for some days. This is known as 'a shibagi chengjel and chak-puba'.[7]

Subsequent to their adoption of Manipuri Yumnak and Shageis, it has become difficult to trace the original clans of the Pangals. Even the local converts either lost their original yumnaks or adopted it after conversion[8] Some Manipuri speaking Muslims possess no sagei-newcomers, like Afghans, Bengalee Muslims, Bihari Muslims etc. There is a group of Manipuri Muslims 'Funga-nai' household slaves who embraced Islam and married amongst themselves.[9]

In an Agrarian based Economy State like Manipur, the family is a major institution of domestic life, and the Meitei Pangals are a family community. Most of the men engaged in agriculture and allied occupations, and the family of a Manipuri Muslim has a special economic significance. Apart from serving as a home for his wife and his numerous children, his aged parents, and perhaps other relations (as in a joint family), the family is an indispensable factor in farm economy. Nearly every member contributes in some way to the process of agricultural production. Especially useful, is the wife's role in the process of agricultural production.

Women's labour is used extensively in agricultural activities like cultivation of rice and vegetables. They constitute almost half of the total agricultural labour force in the rural areas. (Muslim habitation is mainly rural-based) Their labour is used specially in cultivation activities like broad casting of rice seeds, and its transplantation, sowing and reaping of the harvest, threshing, drying of the paddy etc. In addition, they tend and manage vegetable gardens, attached to their homesteads, the productions of which are supplied to the local markets. They also engage in animal husbandry, and poultry farming.

A significant aspect of the Muslim social system is a certain love and regard for parents, which is reciprocal, for the parents in turn, are very solicitous and unduly affectionate. Great respect is accorded to elders, especially religious divines, teachers and scholars. They are addressed with the salutation 'Salam', and are called not by name, but by terms such as 'Chacha', 'Mama', 'Khura', etc.[10]

The most conspicuous events of domestic life, particularly in a rural-agrarian community, were naturally the various stages of growth in the life of a person viz. birth, adolescence, marriage and death, together with the various customs elaborated around them. All these customs had been elaborated with scrupulous regard to every detail. Religious emotion found its best expression in them. Society even judged the respectability of a person by the amount of care and attention given to the fulfillment of this social and religious rites.To begins with: the birth of a child in a family was an event of great importance.[11] A Muslim child when born is welcomed with 'Akamat' i.e. the new-born is made to hear the eternal truth that 'God is one, Mohammad is the last prophet of Islam', and so on. This 'Azan' (prayer) is to be recited in the ear of the child. Later the baby is given its first bath. On completion of seven days, 'Luk Okpa' i.e. the first clean shaving is given to the new-born. Within forty days, able parents offer 'Akika' – they celebrate the coming of the newborn. The parents give the child a suitable name.[12] In fact, among the Pangals, every new born child is given a name in a ceremony that may be performed on any convenient day, but usually before the age of his or her schooling. The name of the child is given by a family member. On the day of naming, the father performs a sacrifice of an animal, a cow or goat, in the name of god. This celebration is known as 'Agiga' among the Imphal area Muslims, and 'Hakhikat' among the Bishnupur and Thoubal Muslims.[13] Meanwhile, the mother of the newborn is confined within the house for a period of forty days, known as 'Chakmangba', she usually dines on rice, dried fish and salt during this period. (Adoption of the Meitei custom) On the completion of forty days, she is permitted to bathe, and then dine in the common dining hall. Subsequently, she is allowed to move to her father's house with the new baby, and be warmly received by her parents who regard the birth of the baby as symbolizing their daughter's permanent place in her husband's home 'Kabak Afaba', 'Changsi Lafai', etc. are presented to the father-in-law by the bride groom's family. The neighbours celebrate the baby's arrival in the maternal uncle's house. When the baby grows, he or she learns the language of his or her mother. When the child attain the age of four, a boy is sent to the village maktab in the morning to learn Arabic, and the fundamentals of Islam. Simultaneously, the child starts going to formal school. For girls, when they attain the age of ten or eleven, they are taught to weave-phanek, khudei, faijom, etc. It is a compulsory skill that a girl has to master before her marriage. Otherwise, she is likely to be neglected by a bride groom's party in search of a bride.[14]

EDUCATION

Islam attaches immense importance to the acquisition and extension of 'ilm' or knowledge. The Quran, the Ahadith and the other sciences are the only road to the understanding of truth. The 'Surah-i-Iqra' opens with an injunction addressed to the prophet to 'Read', and the place assigned to education in Islam can be best appreciated in the light of importance attached to 'ink','pen' and 'paper'. The Prophet recommended education as meritorious in the eyes of the almighty. He made learning compulsory for all the faithful. A Hadith of the Prophet states: 'People cannot do a greater good to their children, than to train and educate them properly'. And stressing the importance of properly educating girls, the Prophets say, 'If a person has daughters or sisters and he treats them properly, and arranges their marriage after they grow up, Allah will reward him with paradise'. The most important duty of parents is to impart education to their offspring.[15]

Muslim education endeavored to achieve two basic aims- religious and secular. But according to Kutub Ahmed Mazumdar, the Manipuri Muslims were completely inclined towards theological studies, which dominated their thinking and moulded their perspective. The Maulanas carved a special niche for themselves in society.[16] The religious aim of education included the study of the Quran as a source or basis of knowledge, and the study of sectarian, moral and spiritual disciplines including the basic articles of faith. Secular aims included the synthesis of secular knowledge and religious belief, the conception and extensive practice of equal educational opportunities, And the establishment of teachers as guides and authorities in forms of knowledge, based upon revelation or direct injunction. In fact, it was the practical aims of Muslim secular education which was responsible for application of technological expertise to the development of irrigation systems, textile manufacture, iron and steel products etc.[17]

In Manipur, the rulers of the state were quite indifferent to the need for education, and the first school established by the British, was a failure. Most of the high officials and darbar members did not know how to read and write, and were content to maintain the status quo. In fact, the Maharajas of Manipur did not favor education, as they feared that their subjects once educated, may demand concessions in various spheres which they were not willing to concede. Learning was confined mainly to the traditional priestly class, and the Brahmins. The pupils had to go to the houses of Maichous (scholars) for learning scriptures.[18] A Different view is presented by Jamini Devi. 'The modern system of education was introduced in Manipur in the later part of the nineteenth century. Before the advent of the system, Manipur had her own indigenous system of education, which emphasized all round development of a person, rather than imparting literacy; most of the knowledge was transmitted orally form one generation to the next before the art of writing and printing were introduced. Parents were mainly responsible for imparting knowledge to the children, and family was the main agency of education. The ancient kings of Manipur were great patrons of learning, physical culture, art and literature; Manipur had their own scripts in writing books. Using this script, scholars of ancient Manipuri wrote books on different subjects. There was no organised form of schools in those days. However, Maiba Loishang, Pandit Loishang, Pannah Loishang, served the purpose of the school in an informal way; Kangla (erstwhile capital) was a great centre of learning. Every house of the Gurus was a school in a sense'.[19]

The education of women was not neglected in ancient Manipur. Parents were mostly responsible for imparting education to their daughters. Young girls were trained in etiquette, court language, administration and even martial arts. Mothers imparted training to their daughter in embroidery, weaving, and domestic matters. The girls attended Sinaipham, where groups of girls did spinning, embroidery and weaving. Sinaipham was a school for girls in a sense. While attending Sinaipham, the girls learned in groups'- manners, customs, etiquette, besides the particular skill, art. Every attempt was made to infuse the spirit of piety and religious formalities, , and spiritual atmosphere among the growing youths, both boys and girls.[20] The Muslim in Manipur emulated the Meiteis in imparting skill in embroidery and weaving, and knowledge of religion, to their daughters.

Following the Muslim settlement in the early seventeenth century, King Khagemba permitted Mohammad Sani, the Qazi and Shanglakpa to attend the Darbar. The latter was fluent in Bengali and Urdu, and was entrusted with translating messages from Taraf into Meiteilon.[21] This was the first official use of the education of a Manipuri Muslim. Despite this promising start, the Meitei-Pangal, did not give much importance to Education, more particularly, Western Education.[22]

In the seventeenth century, the Meitei Pangals might have learnt Meteilon, writing it in the Bengali script, from persons such as Muhammad Sani, Syed

Ambiya, Syed Abdullah, Syed Hussein, Sheikh Zunneid/ Chuleiya, Sifar Muhammad Sheikh Seijanat, Syed Siliman (Suleiman), Syed Ngangba, Sheikh Noori. There was a Lairikyengbam clan (learned in writing and reading) among the Meitei-Pangal. Religious education was imparted by Munshis, Sayeds, and Saints. Some learned wrote Tawiz (notation in Arabic/Urdu for a patient) The Muslims believed that the learning of English would defile the purity of their creed. So it came about, that education among the Muslims, was confined in the initial stags to the learning of Arabic, Urdu and the knowledge of the Quran. They received education form the Madrassahs. The years 1907-08, were a landmark in the history of education of the Muslims in Manipur. In these two years, a madrasah was established at Lilong, whose curriculum included Arabic, Urdu and Persian. Because of the trio of classical languages taught, the Number of boys attending the school trebled in a year, And An additional maulvi had to be provided for in the next year's budget .The real start of muslim education in the state began with the appearance of the Maulvis, who returned after study to Manipur in 1910. They were Mohammad Abdul Jalil of Thoubal, Mohammad Ebadullah of Irong, Mohammad Usman Gani of Keikhu, Mohammad Hafis Ali and Mohammad Moinuddin also of Thoubal, Mohammad Omedalli, Mohammad Sarfuddin and Mohammad Bro Mia of Haoreibi.[23] They were too few in number to satisfy the aspirations of the Muslims for education. Whereas one Maulvi, UsmanGani, settled at Imphal, others settled in villages, and education of the Muslim spread to the rural country side. The Muslim pupils were taught in Arabic, Urdu and Parsee (Farsi), to facilate knowledge and understanding of the importance of Kalima, Namaz, Roza, Haj and Zakat.

The first Maulvi Ebadullah imparted free education. But with the appearance of madrassahs, Education became more formally oriented.Yet the growth of Madrassas was slow and inadequate, and education of Muslims remained confined to a few. Although some Muslims went outside Manipur to study, a few students made their entry in UP schools, patterned on the western model. Maulvi Saraf Uddin Ahmed Khan established a madrassah in the reign of Maharaj Churachand, which taught both the English language, and the Art of writing. He also admitted female students. Of 66 LP schools in the valley, only four were Madrassahs in 1911-12. The Faiza M.E. Madrassah was established in 1935-36. Lilong however, had the highest number of primary schools, with a literacy rate of 35.57 in 1981, of which 14.29% were girls.[24] Generally speaking, education of women was not recognised as essential, apart from theological reasons, and Men's Education remained a priority, especially as women were confined to domestic chores and agricultural duties. Education of girls was limited to the recitation of the Holy Quran, learning how to become a dutiful wife and responsible mother, and being conscientious with reference to religious obligations. With the passage of time, and after Manipur's merger with India (1949), Muslim understood the significant benefits of education, and children were encouraged to go to schools and colleges. In the initial phase, only males could attend Educational institutions, with only a few girls, mainly the daughters of educated parents[25].

The changing attitude of the community towards education is evident from the increasing number of school and college going students, both male and female, not only within but also outside the state. Of the total persons staying outside the state for education of male and female students the ratio is 86.36% and 13.64% respectively[26]. The table of Literacy rate of Muslims according to the 2001 census is – in rural areas male literacy 72.1 and female literacy 37.7, in urban areas, male literacy 82.2 and female literacy 51.0. This may be contrasted with the results of 1981; the pass percentage of Muslim students at the High School Leaving Examination stood at only 1.66% and 0.73% at the Higher Secondary level in 1989[27].

In order to achieve the goal of universal elementary education by 2010, the government has been trying to improve access to education by ensuring availability of schools to all, within a reasonable distance from habitations, and reducing the direct and indirect cost of education through schemes like free books, midday meals, free education etc. The universalization of elementary education Sarva Shiksha Abhiyan, seeks to ensure the enrolment of all children in the age group of six to fourteen years in schools. A picture of the children belonging to Meitei-Pangal community of Manipur, enrolled upto 2004 may be seen from the following table:-

Out of the total students currently enrolled in the government schools, only 7.50% were found in the pre-primary level, as against 17.39% in private schools. In totality, the pre-primary school going students constitute 12.87%. Of the total number of ever enrolled

Enrolment Status	*Imphal East*	*Imphal West*	*Bishnupur*	*Thoubal*	*Churachandpur*	*Chandel*	*Total*
Ever	5,408	3776	2,843	17,321	105	327	39,780
Enrolled	(78.37)	(67.99)	(60.20)	(78.39)	(70.95)	(60.11)	(75.44)
Not	4,253	1778	1,880	4,776	43	217	12,947
Enrolled	(21.63)	(32.01)	(39.80)	(21.61)	(29.05)	(39.89)	(24.56)
Total child population	19,661	5,554	4,723	22,097	148	544	52,727
Aged 5-14 years	100,00	100.00	100.00	100.00	100.00	100.00	100.00

children in the government as well as private schools, the highest number enrolled is in the primary level (Class I to V) which constitutes 62.07%. It is followed by the middle (VI to VIII) with 20.07%, pre-primary 12.87% secondary level (IX to X) constitute only 4.99%, 45.7% of the students are enrolled in government schools, while 54.3% in private schools[28].

Girls educations lags behind that of boys. The average years of schooling for a Muslim girl is five years; there is greater enrollment in urban areas.[29] Muslims of Manipur in contrast to non-Muslims in the state, did not encourage women's education. Males took charge, and presided over family matters, and provided for the family, as girls after marriage moved out of their natal homes. Poverty and lack of functional need also acted as impediments to women's education. While the states female literacy rate is 47.6% that of Muslim women is as low as 5%. Few could proceed beyond the high school level. In rural areas, they often suffered from reverted relapsed illiteracy. Upto 1998, there were only four Muslim women who were post-graduates. (Two are serving as lecturers) Up to 1995, there were only 5704 matriculates, 1822 graduates and 86 technical and Professional graduates. Naturally, due to social and educational backwardness, Muslim women have a low level of political participation, which in turn has limited their role in decision- making. Due to this lack of political articulation, the Muslim women exercise their franchise, according to the directives of the male heads of their families[30].

In Manipur, women did not learn much before the war. Only a few women learnt to read the Quran in

Arabic, and the Hadith in Urdu. Young girls of four to five years attended madrassas, maktabs to study religious books and the Manipuri language. As there were no middle high Schools in Muslim concentrated areas there was a high drop-out of girl students. In 1950, the number was reduced to four out of fifteen-twenty girls at Hatta, and three at Babupara. In rural areas, there were no girl students. In 1952, some girls began to study at nearby schools. In 1955, only two girls passed matric and attended college. In 1956, two girls also cleared matric. One completed her graduation (B.A.) in 1959, one girl completed graduation in Arts, and two in 1960. The first M.A. Degree holder emerged in 1963. By 1979-80, more than twenty girls had completed their Masters and more their graduation. In 1965, the first Muslim girl was admitted in the prestigious G.P. Women's college. The admission of girls in the Science Graduate Programme was negligible. There are no girls' government schools and colleges in Muslim dominated areas like Kshetrigao, Hatta, Kairang, Sangai Yumpham, Sora and kwakta, but there are government higher schools in Yairipok, Lilong Haoreibi, Moijing and Irong. For purposes of higher education, girls have to go to urban areas, these lead to financial and socio-cultural problems.[31]

Currently both Muslim men and women are realising the importance of education, but not to the same extent. They no longer confine children to madrassahs, but enroll them not only in government institutions, but Christian Missionary schools and other private establishments. The students follow the established state or central government (CBSE) curriculum. As an incentive to the 'girl child', scholarships are provided to poor Muslim girls, through the Waqf Board. Schooling is generally not free, but a few madrassahs provide free education to girls. The madrssahs are funded by donations from the Muslim community; a house hold donation is taken out annually at the time of 'jalsa'. The State Waqf Board and Central Waqf council also fund madrassahs. A few non-formal, adult literacy programmes have been set up, but their performance needs improvement even though some non-governmental organisations are doing exemplary work in this field. Limited programmes on the issues of forced marriages, legal rights etc. are held by organistions like the Islamic Social Educational Cultural Development Organisation (Bishnupur district) and Rural Social and Educational Development Association (Mayang Imphal)[32].

Among the group of five to fourteen years surveyed, parents were reticent on the reason why 67% of children did not attend school 13% did not enroll in any school as their parents were not interested in schooling, and 9% refrained, to enable them to participate in household economic activities, whereas 2% could not enroll because of the question of affordability. Of a total of 52,727children 39,780 children were reported to have enrolled; children never enrolled constitute 32.55% of the total child population of the age group five to fourteen years. The dropout rate among the enrolled is 9.68% (due to pressure of household activities) as the family income increases, the number of students receiving the free midday meal decreases. The overall number of students studying in the pre-primary and primary levels in the government schools, under the caption 'free of cost' was found to be 6731. Majority of the students go on foot to schools, which is easily accessible. School buses are not common.[33]

The educational system largely being theologically inclined instilled moral values into students. But it also impacted social participation of Muslims in traditional customs and ceremonies of the Meitei, as for e.g. 'thabal chongba (community Holi dances), khubak-i-sei (song), dance drama (shumang leela) etc.[34] Earlier Muslims actively participated in such events, but from the twentieth century, when more emphasis was placed on strictly following Quranic injunctions, participation of Muslims fell drastically.

The next most important event in domestic life, after basic education, was the circumcision ceremony of boys ranging from seven to ten years. Known as 'Sunat touba' or 'khatna', it was performed by a 'Napit'. (specialist) In modern times, this procedure is sometimes carried out in the sterile environment of a hospital.

No special ceremony marked a girl's attainment of puberty. On the contrary, certain impositions (taboos) were placed on the girl during the period of ritual impurity (menstruation) these restrictions were similar to those observed by Meitei girls- the Muslim girl had to refrain from 'Namaz' and cooking and could resume these obligations only after ritual ablution.

MARRIAGE

Quite naturally, in a pre-dominant rural society, marriage would occupy an important place. Although there was no fixed limit for the age of marriage until very recently, the Muslims favored early marriage. Conferring the children in marriage, and supervising the attendant customs and ceremonies, was the privilege of parents. Marriage is enjoined as a sacred obligation upon every Muslim. The marriage of their children involved many delicate and complicated problems, For instance, those of family status, Ancestral rites and traditions, social honour of the parties. Parents and relatives usually carried out their responsibilities most scrupulously in every detail, emulating perhaps the Meiteis in this regard. Marriage was more a family question, than a personal concern of the marrying couple. However, the practice of 'chenba'-elopement, prevalent in Meitei society, was practiced by many Muslim couples anxious to wed. This had led Quazi Hamid Ali to conclude that the marriage system of the Manipuri Muslims is a combination of Islamic and Manipuri customs.[35] It is difficult to provide a comprehensive description of marriage ceremonies, considering that so many weighty social considerations made it, the most conspicuous event of domestic life. Marriage through negotiation and mutual agreement was common. The marriage date was decided, based on convenience.[36] A stage was generally reached in marriage negotiations, when the parties agreed to the wedding of two individuals, the future bride and bridegroom. This agreement was celebrated with suitable ceremonies. Although elopement is not permitted by the Quran, the Muslims were influenced by the Meitei practice of 'chengba'. In an elopement, the man took the woman to a friend's residence and spent the night there. In the morning, the father of the intending groom together with his male relatives went to the women's residence and made a proposal for marriage. If it was acceptable, the nikhah was performed on the second night after the elopement either at the residence of the bride or groom. If a negative response was received, the marriage is deferred till an agreement is reached. Marriage among Muslims is a civil contract and like contracts, it cannot be validated under duress. Essentially, it is a relation of love, based on the spouse's willingness to have the union, and it is supposed to strengthen faith, and to further the cause of Islam.[37] It is known as 'Nikah'.

There are certain forbidden categories of women that a Muslim man cannot marry. The Meitei-Pangal, however, follows the practice of not marrying either a close relative or a clan member, although these do not fall within the prohibited categories. The only exception is marriage between cross-cousins i.e. brother's son and sister's daughter and vice-versa, but it is not a popular practice. The Pangals abstain from marrying into their own clan for fear of adverse consequences, like congenital defects; malformed, deformed or mentally and physically retarded children. This practice bears the imprint of Meitei custom. During King Charairongba's reign, A certain clan 'Meraimayum' was wiped out, except for one unborn child, because of the crime of arranging an endogamous marriage[38]. There are a few exceptions to marrying in one's own clan.

Although the Quran permits a man to take four wives provided all are treated equally, polygamy is not much practiced in the Meitei Pangal community. The number of male Meitei-Pangals is 1,01,966 and of females 1,00,389 respectively.[39] So the conditions that prevailed in the early days of Islam, when men were warriors and waged wars resulting in a decimation of male population and the incidence of polygamy is not relevant to Meitei-Pangal society. The holy Quran has imposed strict conditions for marrying several wives. "And if you fear that you will not deal fairly by the orphans, marry of women who seem good to you, two or three or four, and if fear that you cannot be fair to so many then one only or (captives) that your right hand possess. Thus it is more likely that you will not do injustice'. Another verse says: 'you will not be able to deal fairly between your wives, however much you wish, You do not turn completely aside (from one), so that you leave another in suspense, if you maintain proper conduct and do your duty, Allah is ever forgiving and merciful (4:129).

In certain circumstances however, a man is permitted to take another wife. If the first wife is barren and the husband desires to have children, or if the wife is chronically ill, unable to discharge her marital and household duties or if the number of women far outshines the number of men, marriage to another women is permitted.[40] In the Event of a subsequent marriage, the husband violates the law, if he does not first seek the consent of his first wife (wives) to marry the other. In any case, the incidence of polygamy is extremely low in Manipur, perhaps for financial reasons, (the Muslims are economically backward); A small percentage of Muslims practice it, mainly in Imphal. But second or subsequent wives are all accorded respect, and sometimes even exercise or exert more influence over the husband, than the first wife. Marriage to more than one woman is usually a measure of prestige and standing in society.

In Meitei-Pangal society, widow, widowers and divorcees are permitted to remarry. Marriages of the first had to be performed from their natal homes. With reference to the relation between wife and husband: 'A Muslim woman is obedient to her husband not because of an inferiority, but because she accepts him as her guardian.[41] There are a few instances of sororate and leviratic marriages, but they are not common.[42]

Once the decision to marry had been arrived at, either by the parent of the intending couple, or by the couple themselves, certain picturesque ceremonies followed, primarily consisting of "Sagei Kwa Yenba", "Kwa Khaiba" and "Panuka Puba". These are preceded by the 'Haijaba'. The guardian of the bridegroom through the agency of a person known as 'tuti' finds out whether the girl they have chosen as the bride is willing to enter into marriage.

If the girls' guardian answers in the affirmative, a proposal for marriage viz haijaba is made by the bridegroom's guardian. After this preliminary rite, the boy's guardian calls on the girl's parents a second time, to finalise the date for the wedding, As also fix the 'Mehr' (bride-price) "The Mehr is a guarantee in the form of cash or other property, which the wife receives from her Husband in case of dissolution of marriage. Its amount is not fixed, and depends on the Socio-Economic status of the parties concerned.[43] Following the fixation of marriage date and amount of mehr a ceremony known as 'Waroipot' is performed; this Ritual bears the hallmark of Manipuri culture and tradition. It would appear that the Pangals referred to Waroipot as 'Kwa Khaiba'. This follows Sagei Kwa Yenba, which primarily consists of offering of betel-Nut and leaves, by the bridegrooms' father, distributed among the sagei relatives of the girl. The 'Kwa Khaiba' (cutting of betel nuts into four square pieces) is performed on a date agreed to between the parents of bride and groom. After the assembling of the invitees', one or two of the old ladies present, remove the skin of green betel nuts, and cut them into four pieces. If the pieces are found to be without blemish, it is considered as a good omen. After this ritual, betel nuts with leaves as also sweets, brought by the bridegroom's family, are distributed to all invitees in the gathering. This symbolises a formal declaration of the agreement arrived at between the bride and bridegroom's families, with regard to the marriage of their children.[44]

On the day preceding the marriage, 'Panuka Puba' is performed. This ceremony again is akin to the 'Heijapot Puba' of the Meitei. In former days the groom's party carried pan (betel leaf) and Kwa (betel- nut) in small packets called 'Putla' to the bride's residence. A special share of the 'pan' and 'Kwa' was reserved for the bride and her friends. (In those days ladies used pan to stain their lips with colour, As no lipstick was available).[45] At the present juncture pan and Kwa are accompanied by sweetmeats and fruits and distributed to all assembled at the bride's residence, but as was traditional, a special portion (the choicest) of the offering was kept aside for the bride and her companions. Sagei Kwa Chatpa follows- i.e., distribution of invitations for the nuptials to the bridegroom's relatives.[46]

Previously on the day before the wedding, competitive, entertaining sports such as Mukna, Yubilakpi, and Mukna-Kangjei were held between the relatives of the bridal couple. At night, a group dance in essence the Meitei, Thabal Chongba, was performed by friend of both parties. This dance was known as 'Purjak' and was accompanied by Manipuri Folk songs, sung by professional singers.[47]

On the day of marriage, each party prepares lunch for their respective invitees. After the repast, the bridegroom's party proceeds to the bride's Residence.[48] In days gone by, (before the emergence of modern means of transport) the bridegroom's rode a horse, or came attired in a 'Sirvani' and big turban seated in a Palki, his head protected by a large overhead umbrella. However today, recourse is had to cars and buses.[49]

At the commencement of the 'Nikah' the bridegroom is seated on a special cloth-dolaifi. There after the presiding Maulvi who conducts the ceremony summons three males as witnesses. These men are usually the brides' relatives and are known as 'gawaukin'. They repair to the bride's house and provide all particulars of the bridegroom, inclusive of the amount of 'mehr' to the bride- there after she gives her formal consent to the marriage. This formal consent is conveyed to the maulvi who recites the 'khutba' (sermon) intoning verses of the Quran in Arabic. This is followed by a community prayer offered to Allah for the happiness of the Newly-weds. The Nikah complete the bridal couple return to the groom's residence where they reside for a couple of days. They then return to the bride's house and spend an equal number of days-hinamhanba.[50] Just as a wedding feast 'Mapam Chakkouba' is given by a Meitei bride's family on the fifth day consequent to the Marriage the Muslim bridegroom's family hold a grand feast at their residence preferably within three days following the marriage, to which are invited not only relatives of the newly weds but also the poor of the locality. This grand feast is known as 'Waleema'. Waleema in the strict sense of the term may not however be entirely applicable to the Meitei-Pangal marriage feast. Waleema would then have to be performed on the day following the Wedding.

With reference to dowry, the Muslims are considerably influenced by the Meitei concept of 'Awonpot' (gifts given to the bridge by her family). There is no ceiling on the awonpot, and parents generally provide the bride with what is deemed essential to start a happily married life. However, today monetary considerations hold ascendancy over the choice of items given as awonpot, but this phenomenon is common to all communities resident in the state. It is not a particular characteristic of the Pangals alone. However, a charming meaningful custom prevalent among the Muslims is the presentation of a copy of the Quran by the father to the bride on her wedding day. This is a symbolic gesture greatly appreciated.

Mixed Marriages-Although at the beginning of their settlement the Pangals married, Meiteis, the occurrence of such marriages decreased, probably because of the increase in Muslim women. However, even today although same community marriage is preferable, if a Muslim man marries non-Muslim Women, the latter usually converts to Islam, although no force or compulsion can be used to force the women to convert. The children born to such a couple are brought up as Muslim, although they may be given a non- Muslim name. A Muslim woman who marries outside her community is generally looked at askance, but she retains her Right to inherit property.

Death: - Just as with birth, there are certain Rituals associated with death. A dying person is made to lie on a mat spread on the floor, with his head facing north (direction of Kaaba). After death, the mouth is plugged immediately; the eyelids are closed and tied with a white cloth. The two big toes are also tied together with a strip of cloth. Certain terminology is employed to convey the news of a person's death from house to house, and to relatives living elsewhere. The corpse is immediately buried without delay. Cleaning of the dead before burial is important. Some relatives of the deceased bathe the body seven times with hot water boiled, using a special type of leaf, locally known as 'Sungbrei'. They clean each and every part of the body, and plug all orifices with clean cotton. The body is then wiped dry with a piece of new cloth and covered with powdered camphor and perfumed oil applied to the hand, feet, and forehead. The body is wrapped in a new white cloth 'kafanfi'. This is made of three pieces for a man and five pieces for a woman. Various kinds of perfumes are sprinkled over the body before the funeral (janaja). The body is then placed in a wooden coffin 'kai' covered with a white cloth. The sons of the deceased and close relatives carry the bier. Women and children are not allowed (As in the Meitei custom) to accompany the funeral procession, or attend prayers for the dead-Janana Namaz. These last rites are held near the grave and presided over by a maulvi or an imam. Thereafter, the corpse is lowered into the grave (kabar). The body is laid on its back with the head facing a westward direction (kibala). To prevent earth from falling on the body, bamboo sticks (WA) are placed across in rows leaving sufficient space for the body. All relatives and friends fill up the grave with handfuls of soil. Its surface is smoothened to the shape of a dome (intrinsic feature of Islamic architecture). At the home of the deceased no food is cooked, and all relatives including the family members, are fed by a group of neighbours, who help them on such occasions. (This is similar to the singlup tradition of the Meitei where neighbours express sympathy and solidarity with the family of the deceased). After some days the kin perform a ceremony inviting relatives and friends to recite the Quran 'tasbi sonba'. Meals are arranged for them. This Quranic recitation is generally held after forty days.

Position of Muslim Women: - In moral terms, the Quran which repeatedly refers to 'believing men' and 'believing women' and to Muslim men and Muslim women, places the two sexes in a position of absolute equality before god.(33:35) But in social terms, women are subordinate to men. In the context of seventh century Arabia, it is true, that Quranic injunction respecting women, doubtless constituted a progressive force. The Quran emphasises the just treatment of women, it prohibits female infanticide and the inheritance of female slaves, and it provides legal protection for women in matters like inheritance or divorce. But women inherit only half of what men do, and they are generally understood as requiring male supervision, as indicated in the following Quranic verse: 'man are in charge of women because Allah hath made one of them to excel the other, and because they spend of their property for the support of women' So good women are the obedient, guarding in secret, that which Allah hath guarded. As for those from whom ye fear rebellions admonish them, and banish them to beds apart, and scourge them. Then, if they obey you, seek not a way against them.[51]

In Manipur, Muslim society is male- dominated and a gender bias exists, even though under the Shariat, Muslim women enjoy equal social standing with men. Moreover, the wife being under the supervision of her husband, has to consult him before making any decision, as husband is the head of the family.[52] In the social sphere, Muslim women in Manipur are at great disadvantage compared to their counterparts in other communities. Rigid patriarchy and social custom and traditions like restriction on movement, early marriage, misuse of personal laws particularly with reference to 'talaq', adoption, and guardianship of children, maintenance and inheritance, have hindered immensely the process of social empowerment of Muslim women. Misusing the Islamic provision of talaq by Muslim husband is a very common practice in Manipuri Muslim society. Even though theoretically a divorced wife is entitled to provisions and maintenance, in reality divorced women hardly get these benefits. They even fail to get back the mehr promised in the nikah-nama.[53]

In Islam, women are treated as equal partners to men, although their duties and responsibilities are different. Men and women complement one another - women's role is largely home centric, and they possess a strong sense of community. Despite the domestic domain being the natural sphere of the woman, women's position is determined by class, upper class women enjoy more privileges and leisure but ordinary women possess a great deal of mobility, necessitated by the necessity of earning a livelihood. Some section of women even enjoy an egalitarian relationship with their husband, and an equal role in decision-making, others are subordinates as they are entirely or largely dependent on their husbands, whereas other enjoys a limited share of autonomy in the decision making process.[54] The first and foremost duty of a Muslim wife is to serve her husband, and to satisfy him morally and physically. She cooks for the family foods which are permitted; she teaches children Islamic etiquette with respect to food, manners, dress etc. She safeguards the family honor, by for instance, preventing free mixing of the sexes. She is to establish cordial elation with in-laws or members of the extended family. But Muslim mother-in –laws are sometimes unjust and cruel to their mous (daughter-in-laws).Similarly; some daughter-in-laws cause rifts in the family. The Husband is thus placed in a quandary. However, the Muslim wife is the queen of the house, She runs it on her husband's earnings, and contributes to the family kitty through her own economic activities.[55]

Yet, there is a structural hierarchy of authority connecting Allah, men and women. Whereas God and men are grammatical subjects and actors, women are objects of action; indeed much of the chapter entitled 'women' (Sura 4: 1-43) consists of God's instructions to men, as to what they should do in respect of women. (Earliest reference to a normative gendered division of labor is found in a Bengali version of the story of Adam and Eve, dating from the late sixteenth century). In Saiyid Sultan's epic poem 'Nabi Bamsa' the angel Gabriel gives Adam a plow, a yoke, seed and two bulls, advising him that Niranjan/has commanded that agriculture will be your destiny. Adam then planted the seed and harvested the crop. At the same time Eve is given fire with which she learns the art of cooking. In short a domestic life would be Eve's destiny just as Adam's vocation would be farming.[56] The major portion of Manipuri Muslim women do not display any vestige of independent thinking, although most work even outside the home they do not earn enough for a sustainable livelihood.

Women, most of whom reside in the rural areas are largely confined to the domestic domain and prevented from intermingling freely with men. Women's primary duty is to please her husband and responsibly perform her domestic duties. She can then be adjudged 'A good wife'. She is entitled to affection and respect not only from her husband, but also from her children, and the love of children for the mother is very real, and a source of consolation in times of strife. The mother takes upon herself the responsibility of instructing her children in the path of goodness, and imparting to them a sound moral character.

In recent times, in the quest for an identity, greater emphasis has been placed on Quranic injunctions, and women's mobility has been restricted by the adoption of the purdah system. In the medieval period when Muslim rule was established in the country, respectable ladies both Muslim and Hindu shielded their appearance from public scrutiny by using veil- purdah. But Muslim women in Manipur did not ascribe to this custom. Most of them lived on the level of subsistence, and worked to contribute to the family kitty by pursuing an occupation (usually as unlicensed vendors, domestic maids, cultivators etc.) They were unable to cover themselves with a veil, because this would have retarded their ability to work, and impacted their meager income. But as a gesture of respectability, they covered their heads with an inaphi (shawl) which also covered the upper part of their bodies. Some burqa clad women can be seen, but by and large the practice has not taken root in the Pangal community.

Many or most Pangal women cannot trace their genealogy back to the seventeenth century, when the first Muslim settlers were given Meitei ladies to marry by the king. Nevertheless, they share many common traits with Meitei women, and dwell together in harmony, "Hindu and Muslim relations in Manipur are a lodestar for the rest of India. The Muslims in the land came from out side, found wives among the local women folk, and settled down. The Maharaja did not treat them as aliens[57] Muslim women dress as the Meitei-they wrap around themselves a phanek (Sarong), they speak Meiteilon, follow a similar diet (except for abstinence from pork which in any case is not an integral component of Meitei cuisine), live in similarly constructed houses, and multi-task. They jointly participate with Meitei women in programmes and marches, centred on violation of human Right, Economic Empowerment, climatic change, HIV/AIDS, drug use, conservation of the environment etc.

Md. Riyaz Ahmed Shah states that most Manipur Muslim women are hampered by illiteracy, poverty; unreasonable Religio-cultural based confinement at home, devalued position in a male-dominated society, rural habitation where the general mindset is not compatible with the modern Age, lack of information, inability to verify the correctness or reasonability of what they have heard, even on Religious matters.[58]

The mean age of marriage has increased to 22: 5 years, and average number of children borne by a woman is three, rising up to five. Because of changed circumstances, like the emergence of nuclear families, fragmentation of land holdings, inflation, rise in the standard of living, women are now limiting their families and adopting modern methods of family planning. But in general, family planning is not acceptable to the Muslims, 'as they are not well informed about the new sophisticated tools and techniques, and scientific methods of birth control'.[59]

Mehr - This forms for a woman an integral part of the pre-marriage rituals. There is no fixed amount stipulated for the Mehr, the amount being dependent on the social status and financial means of the groom. Obviously, a larger amount would enhance socio-economic status. The mehr once given becomes the exclusive property of the bride who can use it in any manner she sees fit- if so desired, she may share a portion of it with her husband. The objective of giving mehr would appear to be two fold-it accords respect and dignity to the woman and also provides financial security; secondly it acts as a deterrent on the husband, preventing him from arbitrarily dissolving the marriage. In this connection Ashgar Ali Engineer cited the example of the Second Caliph viz. Umar, who wanted to place a ceiling on mehr. He was dissuaded from this action by a woman who recited the Quranic verse: 'And if you had given one of them a heap of gold, take nothing from it.' This verse cautions a husband against appropriating even a miniscule part of the bride price.[60] Mehr is sometimes allowed to be retained by the husband with the wife's consent. In practice the 'mehr' is often symbolic.

Divorce – Marriage being a sacred union, divorce is only permitted when it becomes impossible for the couple to live together in harmony and peace. 'Talaq' which is permissible under certain circumstances is an Arabic word, implying 'freeing' or undoing of knot'. The Quran justifies divorce: "and if you fear that the two may not be able to keep the limits ordered by Allah, there is no blame on either of them, for what she gives up to become free thereby. Marriage is a civil contract, entailing both rights and responsibilities, and the prophet stated "Never did Allah allow anything more hateful to him than divorce. If talaq is given without any reason it is stupidity and ingratitude to God". But being a civil contract marriage is dissoluble under certain circumstances. But, undesirable practices have arisen, where in men divorce their wives for flimsy or arbitrary reasons. In some instances, divorcees (men) force their ex-wives to resume marriage without the latter having married another man. As this is not permissible the former temporarily engages another to marry his ex-wife and then to divorce her after the lapse of a few days. Such marriages are disparagingly referred to as 'nikah khutnek' by the Pangals. After the dissolution of the 'temporary convenience' marriage, the first husband can once again marry his ex-wife. Unfortunately, children born from such unions face social stigma and are barred from becoming 'imams'.

A period of 'iddat' is observed by a woman subsequent to a divorce. During this period of three months, the ex-husband has to provide maintenance for his former wife. In practice, this provision is rarely complied with.

Although it is comparatively easier for a man to seek talaq, a woman is permitted to divorce in particular circumstances. The system prevalent in Manipur is "kabinama" or the penning of a document by the wife laying down certain conditions: if these conditions are not abided by, the marriage is terminated. Such a document tends to restrain a husband from arbitrarily exercising his power to divorce his wife. Even then, if a divorce results, the man is bound to pay something, either in cash or kind to his ex-wife.[61]

The religious law of Islam permits a husband to unilaterally and extra judicially dissolve his marriage, by the simple pronouncement of the formula of divorce. The object of talaq is not to cause distress or heap humiliation on the woman. Simply put, a husband can state in the presence of two witnesses that he is divorcing his wife. Just as is prevalent in other communities, the prime reasons for divorce are infidelity, violence against women, incompatibility, and inability to satisfy dowry demand, chronic illness, and infertility. A Muslim woman can initiate divorce if her husband has disappeared for a period of four years or more, if she has been denied maintenance for two or more years. if the husband has been imprisoned for over seven years, if he has failed to discharge his marital obligations for three or more years, and for reasons such as impotency, insanity leprosy, virulent venereal disease, cruelty, and the wife's desire to observe option of 'puberty' (in case she had been married before the age of fifteen.[62]

The main reasons ascribed for divorce in Manipur are according to one writer-lack of understanding between husband and wife (common in early marriages,) barrenness, and lack of good relationship with the in-laws.[63]

The Pangals adhere to the Hanafi School of jurisprudence. Three forms of talaq are permitted -talaq-e-Ahsan, and talaq-e-hasan and talaq-ul-bidat. In the first instance, the husband pronounces a single talaq, and abstains from marital relations for a period of three months, during which period, reconciliation is possible and divorce is revocable. If this happens the divorce is nullified and marriage is resumed. If talaq is not revoked before the expiry of three months, it becomes final and irrevocable. In the second form of talaq, Talaq-e-Hasan, three separate pronouncements are made at intervals. In this form too, reconciliation and resumption of marriage is permitted before the third pronouncement of talaq. Talaq-ul-widdat is pronouncement of talaq thrice simultaneously -it is final and irrevocable.[64]

Talaq consists of two written documents, containing separate signatures of the husband, wife, drafter of the document and the witness. Copies of the Talaq are retained separately by husband and wife, and produced if required at the time of remarriage. A Muslim woman is barred fron initiating Talaq or making a proposal for reunion with her divorced husband.

According to M.N. Srinivas divestiture (Khul) and dismissal (talaq) are practiced by Muslims: The former entails a friendly agreement between husband and wife, and returning the mehr to the husband, the latter is triple pronouncement of talaq.[65] If after the second pronouncement of talaq, marriage is resumed, it is on equitable terms, where the woman's honor and dignity is safe guarded. Whatever can be done must be done to prevent dissolution of marriage. 'Arbitrators' play an important role and act on behalf of both parties to effect reconciliation.

Divorce can be made by mutual consent or agreement between husband and wife. This is termed as 'Khula' or 'Mubarat' but such divorces are rare.[66]

Sageis: - In its early home in Arabia, Islam believed in perfect democracy, people claimed equality in social as well as political affairs. The Prophet declared in his last sermon: 'know that every Muslim is the brother of every other Muslim. Ye are all a fraternity, all equal.[67] When however, kingship entered Islam and became entrenched (in the medieval period) stratification of society took place. The stratification of Manipuri Muslim society was very different to the stratification of Indian society in the medieval period. Mohammad

Latif Shah writes: "All sections of the Pangal community are not equal in their social status within the society; however, they have no distinct social divisions except for lineages (sageis). The names of these sagei were given by earlier kings of Manipur, on the basis of skill and aptitude. There is no hierarchical differentiation within the sagei, based upon either economy or occupation.[68]

The Manipuri Muslim society possesses some unique features Right from its inception in 1606, Muslims were assigned sageis. It was in recognition of their aptitude for, and interest in specific type of professions, that the Muslims of Manipur were given suitable names of sageis (clans) according to the Loyomba Sinyen, a book on the division of people according to profession. There are about fifty such Muslim clans in Manipur-an exclusive feature, quite unknown in the Muslim world.[69] N. Devendra Singh states that there are thirty-eight yumnaks of Pangals in Manipur. They are:-Ipham, Khulakpam, Khutheibam, Makak Mayum, Sangom Sumbam,Meerai Mayum, Yumkhaibam, Kori Mayum, Aribam, Hawai Ingkhol, Sairem, Moijing, Leishangkhong, Sajaubam, Urup Mayum, Maibam, Thoubal Mayum, Moinam Chesam, Mayang Mayum, Mushera, Phundrei Mayum, Nongjai Mayum, Bhagi Mayum, Thongkhong Mayum, Nongshai Mayum, Shingar Khongbam, Mansham, Keinou Mayum, Kamal Mayum, Makak Mayum Amuba, Bashi Mayum, Mayang Mayum, Phusham, Yangkhubam, Pukhri Mayum, Dolai Pabam and Oinam. The names of sub-clans given on the basis of occupation, post and place of settlement are-Aribam, Mirai Mayum, Makak- Mayum,

Nonjai Mayum, Khullakpam, Bhukra Mayum, Bagi Mayum, Chesam, Phundrei Mayum, Ipham Maibam (Meitei convert), Thoubal Mayum (settled Thoubal), Sajaubam, Phusham, Urup Mayum, Maibam (descendants of Maiba), Thoubal Mayum (settled on banks of Thoubal river), Moinam, Mushara, Mayang Mayum, Nongjai Mayum, Thongkhong Mayum, Nongshayaibam, Shinga Khongbam, Mansham, Keinou Mayum, Makak Mayum Angouba, Kamal Mayum, Bashi Mayum, Mayang Mayum, Phusham, Yangkhubam, Pukhri Mayum, Dolai Pabam and Oinam.

Some of the names of the clans are the same as those assigned to sub-clans. The Muslim migration which commenced in king Khagemba's reign (1596-1652) continued upto the time of King Gambhir Singh (1826-1834) most of these Muslims were from Sylhet, Gouradesh and Shirihata.[70]

W.Ibohal also concurs with the theory that family title or 'yumnak sagei' was assigned on the basis of occupation-this is explicit from the titles themselves. Some sageis assigned on this basis were as follows. The Phundrei sageis operated an implement known as 'lathe' and were proficient in carpentry. This clan in collaboration with Khuleibam and Korimayum clans, made an artistic palanquin fitted with seven lotus leaves made of ivory, richly decorated and inlaid with gold and silver, its two sides being covered with copper (Pangan Thoklakpa, Nong Samei) Another Muslim clan Dolaipabam was also connected with Dolaipaba Loisang (department of palanquins).The use of palanquins commenced from that time. The Phundrei clan was entrusted with the art of making or turning the hookah

-neck flagtip, paytip, tool leg, horai (dishes), bookstand, basket leg, charkha etc. Kandan of khuleibam clan manufactured a device for pressing sugarcane. Nooria Sheikh of the Phusam (potter) clan manufactured an exquisite pot-sanahal, through the wheeling technique, and presented it to the king. Pottery was one of the principal trades of the Muslims. The Maibam (physician) clan practiced the curative profession. The physician was at the same time 'a magician and sooth sayer'. The Chesam clan is credited with introducing the art of manufacturing paper. The Phisam (weaver) clan made distinctive fabrics on the traditional loom-dolaiphi, kangthol phitha etc. exclusive to the Muslims. The Muslims produced good quality silk at Ahong Ingkhol. They may have brought this craftsmanship from Bengal, as according to the Ain-i-Akbari, in the sarkar of Sonargaon was produced a species of Muslin very fine. Several kinds of fruit seeds, including the mango seed were introduced, and the Muslims opened a garden called 'Ningthem Inkhollen' at Khomidok. Higgins refers to the clan 'Hawai ingkhol' (pulse growers). The Pangal ingkhol clan produced sugar cane juice, flower seeds, coriander, opium etc. The Keikhong Ingkhol clan produced mustard seeds, garlic, and onion. Other Sageis accorded by occupation were 'Sangom Sumbam' or cattle-rearers, whose head had presented a pot of milk sweets to King Khagemba. Shingakhongbam were proficient in playing the Bengoon (clarinet).[71]

Other clan names were given on a different basis. For instance, the descendants of that person who presented a moina bird to King Khagemba were known as 'Moinam' Those who guarded hemp 'Ee' were called

'Eefam', descendants of the person who partioned a 'yum' (house) were termed 'Yumkhaibam', those who settled at Kainow, as Kainow Mayum. Mohammad Sani the chief of the Muslims who came to Manipur in 1606 had three brothers; one became a Khulakpa (administrator of the village), his descendants were known as 'khulakpam'. An individual with a heavy body Shah kusum was known as 'Shajauba', his descendants 'Shajaubam.[72]

Some Sageis were based on place of Residence-Ipham, the Muslims who protected the thatched garden of the royal palace, Moijingmayum-the Muslim who settled in the foot-hills of Moijing in Thoubal, Urup after the settlers at Tengeikha Puruksoubi termed Urup Mayum, Thoubal mayum after those Muslims who left for Thoubal to protect it against Maring raids, Thongkhong Mayum after Muslims who settled near a bridge (possibly Minuthong), Wangmayum after Muslims who settled at Wanajing, Keinou Mayum for a Muslim who settled at Keinou to guard against tigers, Nonajaimayum after Abdul Qarim who settled at Nongchai, Keikhongta after Muslims settled at Keikhu Keikhong to prevent attacks by tigers.

Yet other sagei were assigned on the basis of the nature of administrative duties performed: Dolaipabam (palanquin service), Luplakpam (the kullakpa of a village was assisted by a luplakpa in Paikhomba's reign 1666-1697), Panchai mayum (after the war of 1891, 2 courts were established Cheirap and Panchayat-a Muslim Changemba was appointed as a Panchayet member, Menjor mayum (after the first Muslim who became a Menjor (Major) in the military administration- viz.Thabal in Chandrakirti's reign 1850), Pukri mayum (the Muslim in charge of the king's pukhri-tank-Saikh Jallauddin proficient in catching fish), and Mansam after (a father-son duo of wrestlers Akun Sheikh and Kanba Shah, was appointed to the darbar).

Two sageis were named after the original homeland of the Muslim migrants into Manipur viz. Bhukramayum (Bhukrain Sylhet) and Makak mayum (Makak in Sylhet) A few sageis were ascribed for reasons other than these –Shairem Keisa Miya married a Meitei of the Shairem clan and adopted his wife's clan name Oinammayum. A local Oinam Bira who converted to Islam in Chandrakirti's reign retained his original yumnak. Miraimayum- after Mir Shayeed who came to Manipur in 1609 with thirty- seven members, and presented himself and the others to the King. Bagi Mayum- Purnot captured a Urok (egret-bagah) and gifted it to King Khagemba. Sajoubam- Musaq Ali Mulah, youngest brother of Prasena Langjinglen came in 1623 to see him. He had a well proportioned body – SA- joubam.[73]

The Makak Mayum clan had a further division into Makak Mayum Angouba and Makak Mayum Anuba (fair and dark complexion persons.) In a similar manner Mayang Mayum group was divided into Mayang Mayum Anouba and Ariba (new and old, the former migrated in Chandrakirti's reign, the other in Gambir Singh's.[74]

The Muslim clans have been invariably exogamous. What is permissible under Islamic law- indogamy became almost a dead letter.[75]

W. Ibohal Singh opines that 'nowadays, the Muslim community of the Meiteis hardly uses their family titles. It appears they prefer the Persian style of name.[76] The number of sageis varies in different accounts, but is generally held to be fifty in number.

Muslims in Manipur can be broadly divided into four groups' viz. Sheikh, Sayyid, Pathan and Mughul. The following table is indicative of this classification:-

1. Aribam (Sheikh)
2. Khullakpam (Sheikh)
3. Khutheibam (Sheikh)
4. Phundrei mayum (Pathan)
5. Yumkhaibam (Pathan)
6. Yumkhan (Pathan)
7. Sanggomsumbam (Sheikh)
8. Korimayum (Sheikh)
9. Ayekpam (Sheikh)
10. Hawai-Ingkhol (Sheikh)
11. Phusam (Sheikh)
12. Leishangkhong (Sheikh)
13. Sajabam (Sheikh)
14. Moijing (Sheikh)
15. Urupmayum (Pathan)
16. Maibam (Sheikh)
17. Thoubal mayum (Sheikh)
18. Moinam (Sheikh)
19. Chesam (Sheikh)
20. Mushram (Sheikh)
21. Bogimayum (Sheikh)
22. Sairem (Sheikh)
23. Thongkhongmayum (Sheikh)
24. Wangmayum (Sheikh)

25. Singgakhongbam (Sheikh)
26. Nongjaimayum (Sheikh)
27. Mansam (Sheikh)
28. Phisabam (Sheikh)
29. Kamal mayum (pathan)
30. Pukhri mayum (Sheikh)
31. Dolai pabam (Sheikh)
32. Meraimayum (Sayyid)
33. Baseimayum (Sheikh)
34. Konthamayum (Sheikh)
35. Impham (Pathan)
36. Labuktongbam (Pathan)
37. Makakmayum Angouba (Moghul)
38. Makakmayum Amuba (Moghul)
39. Nongsayaibam (Moghul)
40. Keinoumayum (Pathan)
41. Yangkhubam (Sheikh)
42. Oinam (Sheikh Anouba)
43. Mayang Ariba (Sheikh)
44. Hidak- Ingkhol (Sheikh)
45. Mayang Anouba (Sheikh)
46. Phiringjimayum (Sheikh)
47. Touthongmayum
48. Heibok mayum
49. Keithel – ingkhol
50. Tampak – Mayum[77]

Most clans belong to the 'Sheikh' group. A. Hamid Ali writes that "It is apparent that the word 'sheikh' is common to names of early Muslim settlers. But all such persons were neither religious teachers or heads of orders of darwishes. It might be that some of them were real 'Sheikh' as it was a custom with the Muslim

Governors and Generals to take learned men and Auliyas with them, wherever they went. Other used the word 'Sheikh' as a surname, being sons or descendants of a Sheikh, others used it as part of their name. The Nongshamai describes about the coming of Sayyids and Moghuls during the time of Khagemba and Paikhomba respectively.[78]

Social Stratification: - Stratification in society was based upon occupation. In the early phase of settlement, Some Muslims were absorbed into the king's Army, and their primary occupation consisted of defending the kingdom from external or internal raids. This group of Muslims was known as 'Khunja'. Another group who pursued peaceful vocations such as textile producers, paper makers, carpenters, potters etc. were known as "Ingkhol" or "Ingkhol Shangba".[79] The latter group were more numerous but they enjoyed a lower status; both groups were liable to render lallup (Feudal service). The main duties of Khunja revolved around military services, but this did not excuse them from performing manual labour- this indicates that a measure of equality permeated Muslim society. During period of peace, the numbers of Muslims increased, and a further stratification of the original two groups took place. The Khunja split into two -Moulvi or Munsi (Religious head) and Lanmi (Soldier), the Ingkhol Shangba split into Khut- heiba (artisans) and Ingkhol Sangba (gardeners).

As the word itself denotes- moulvis were primarily assigned religious and educational tasks, which entitled them to enjoy the highest position in Pangal society. Enjoying great respect, they busied themselves with ensuring that all Muslims abided by Quranic injunctions. They also doubled up as teachers in Madrassas. This class of people was exempted from lallup and payment of taxes.

The Lanmi had the responsibility of the defence of the kingdom. They were assigned the task of guarding the Royal palace and granaries in times of peace. When liable to render lallup, they were attached to the Pangal Loisang which assigned them duties. This Loisang was a separate government department, located in the palace compound.

Placed below these two groups in the social hierarchy were the khutheiba, pursuing different vocational trades. As they also had to perform lallup, they were similarly attached to the Pandit Loisang to be engaged in carpentry works, inclusive of boat making. Their services were also utilized in variegated works, such a weaving, road- repairing, bridge – building, dredging of rivers and canals and military duties.

Ingkhol sangba occupied the lowest rung of the social ladder. In lieu of feudal service, they paid an annual tribute to the king. These people were mainly associated with agricultural works and agro-manufactures.[80]

Domestic and Social Comforts: - The vast majority of the Manipuri Muslim resides in villages. Despite their habitation being Rural based, 92.9% of them possess or own land, whereas 3.0% hold government land, more or less on ownership terms. In an agrarian based Economy state 62.0% of Meitei-Pangal householdspossess cultivated land without irrigation facilities, whereas 16% possess uncultivated land. A significant observation made is that all Meitei Pangal households reside in their own buildings. Most of the buildings are in fact 'kutcha houses' (62.0%), only 6.0% Muslims live in pucca buildings, 31.2% in semi-pucca buildings.[81] The housing sector manifested an essential element of Manipur's self-sufficient economy. For building houses only locally available materials –bamboo, timber, thatch, mud, cow dung etc were used. Supply of these needs did not normally involve any market transactions. People of ordinary means built their houses with family- labour and/ or labour of the neighbors on mutual co-operation basis. The well to-do people could engage labour on payment of wages. But the wage rate was not determined by market forces, customary rates prevailed.

Plans and designs of houses were useful and practical rather than decorative. They were also cost effective in terms of both resources and time required for their construction. The framework of a hut was made of bamboos, its walls with locally grown reeds which then were plastered over with mud mixed with cow-dung. The roofs were covered with thatch. People who were better- off used timber and bamboo for erecting the structures of their houses which had the same mud plastered walls and thatched roofs. As for size, their houses and courtyards were of course; much bigger and quality of materials used was better than that used by ordinary people. One reason for avoiding brick houses was that Manipur was Earthquake prone and also, a large section of people could not afford to build houses with bricks.Moreover the houses could be quickly rebuilt following devastations caused by marauders from across the borders.

The plans of houses of different classes of people had some common features. Every house was East-facing, having an open verandah in that direction. There were no windows in the walls. Light and air could enter through just two doors, one opening into the verandah and the other into the north wall near the North-West corner.The big open verandah served as the place where all activities took place in the day time excepting for cooking which was done inside the room which had no partition. The bed side of the head of the family located near the South wall was screened off by mats to ensure privacy.

The houses were environment- friendly, and in pleasant harmony with the natural surroundings. Every house had a fenced-in compound containing gardens of fruit and vegetable plants and a small pond. The water in the pond was kept clean as it was used for drinking. Washing was not done in the pond. For such activities water would be lifted from the pond, and used in a manner that would prevent the soiled water from falling back into the pond. The compound added to the wealth of the community/state, in the shape of recurring annual yields from the kitchen garden, orchard and tank.[82]

In selecting a dwelling site and in the construction of a house, Pangals observe certain Meitei rituals. First, the plot of land is divided into nine parts Langja yumpham (vulture), Phiral yumpham (flag), Meikhu yumpham (smoke) Samu yumpham (elephant) Sangai yumpham (royal site) Nongsa yumpham (lion) Lolla yumpham (ass) Tampha yumpham (diamond) and Lambui yumpham (fox). The first three parts were held as taboo for purposes of construction. The south west portion of the house, known in Meitei dialect as 'Santhong' is regarded as sacred. The south eastern part of the dwelling 'Phamen', is assigned to the head of the family as in Meitei tradition. Emulating the latter, the Muslim also built a 'Sangoi' (Courtyard) either in the east or the north, a 'Kei' – granary, and in earlier times a 'sangol' or stable.[83] Unlike the Meities, the Pangal does not reserve a space in the house for family deity.

Most of the Muslims preferred to settle along river banks, rivulets, streams or the peripheries of lakes. For this reason, availability of water decided their choice of habitat. They were thus enabled to meet their requirements of drinking water from canals, lakes, tanks and ponds. It is interesting to note that with the increase in population, changing climatic conditions, and failure of the state government to provide essential amenities, or maintain them in a proper condition, many Meitei – Pangals, like other communities resident in the state, have to set a part of their earnings to buy water. Access to running water is limited to a very few urban households, but they too are constrained in times of drought (which is frequent) to buy water. Water is a relatively expensive commodity and a great incidence on income. In fact 36.6% of households are dependent for drinking water on rivers and canals. Only 9% of Meitei Pangals have access to taps as a source of drinking water.

For purposes of lighting, majority of the Muslims have resort to kerosene lamps (554 out of 1000) electric power is available to 432 per 1000 households. Similar would be the use of LPG for cooking. Poorer households use kerosene stoves or firewood. With reference to sanitation, 904 out of 1000 families lack Access to a bathroom, and only 66 out of 1000 use Septic tanks. This Abysmal condition is due to the depressed socio-economic status of the Muslims, as also a lack of awareness.

As regards means of transportation, the most popular mode is by bicycle, as it is suited to the rural habitation and is affordable to at least 68% of the households. A miniscule proportion i.e. one percent own jeeps, cars, trucks, buses, whereas three percent own carts (these are especially useful to cart paddy after the harvest) but are today becoming almost obsolete as tractors with an attachment are used to transport paddy.

The Meitei- Pangal spends considerably more on food as opposed to non-food items. As much as 60.7% of total expenditure is incurred on food. The average monthly per capita expenditure is worked out as Rs. 474/- against Rs. 655.86 of rural Manipur in 2004.[84] Food habits are similar to that of the Meitei, and rice forms the staple diet. The famed bread 'Roti' of the Muslims is only taken in the morning along with tea. The different kinds of breads (especially of the moglai cuisine) popular with Muslims elsewhere in the country, especially in north India are not much in demand (e.g. Rumali roti), and Muslim hotels generally serve rice and meat. The Muslim introduced however the eating of 'tan' (bread) in Manipur. However they partake of it only in the morning and it is regarded as a secondary item of diet.[85]

The Pangals like Muslims elsewhere relish meat dishes, but they refrain from eating pork, which is forbidden by the Quran. There is a clear distinction between 'halal' and 'haram', only the first category is consumed by the Pangals. The Muslims however freely partake of vegetables, fish, eggs, herbs, etc. They refrain from eating the 'eel' Fish, commonly sold in the main markets. Non fertilized egg is a favourite food; there is a taboo on fertilized eggs. Some Muslim eat different kinds of meat- beef, mutton and chicken. Buffalo meat is not a part of their diet. The staple food is rice, supplemented by pulses, besides roots and tubers. They also consume seasonal fruits. The drinks primarily consist of milk, tea and other beverages. On festive occasions they take a special food prepared from sugarcane juice viz. chuhi. However some changes in their food habits have occurred due to the impact of urbanization, such as the use of dried or fermented fish.[86] Cows are slaughtered on rare occasions such as feasts, marriage, and other auspicious ceremonies, festivals. Although cow meat is sold on a regular basis by some butchers, the cost of a cow is prohibitive, and therefore its slaughter is limited to occasions when sacrificial offering has to be made to god or to stave off illness, adversity. Sometimes a goat or even a fowl is sacrificed .Grand feasts are also arranged by the heirs of a deceased, to ensure eternal rest for the soul of the deceased. Other instances of animal sacrifice are on occasions like 'Akikah' and 'Eid-ul-Azha, when qurbani is routinely performed, and the meat of the slaughtered animal is distributed to relatives and neighbours.

To the Pangals may be attributed culinary talent evident in the preparation of tasty curries, the taste enhanced by the addition of spices, mustard oil, ginger, garlic etc. They possess special techniques to extract mustard oil and to make spices. Like the Meiteis they prepare 'Khir' (rice pudding) but they also make special sweetmeats and sharbats. They specially relish the Meitei delicacies of 'iromba' and 'Amerpa' (chutney made of chilli and femented fish), which are prepared fresh every day. The use of alcohol and wine is prohibited both by religion and the state.[87] In the immediate past, from the 1990's onwards when heroin become easily available illicit drug use became common to many Muslim youth – drug trafficking is also common. Besides heroin, other drugs of choice are Spasma proxyvon and similar drugs.

Pangal Elders both men and women smoked a hookah from the time of their settlement in Manipur. R.K. Jhaljit Singh writes: 'Tobacco-smoking was introduced into Manipur in 1610, very soon the Manipuris discarded the pipe, and used the hookah to minimize the ill effects of tobacco-smoking. The first hookahs were imported from the Mughal Empire. They were called 'Mangal phoo' (Mughal pot), soon hookahs began to be manufactured in Manipur. The first indigenously made hookah came into use in 1615.[88] Eating of pan, and smoking of bidis (even by women) and cigarettes is also prevalent among the Muslims. Women vendors are especially partial to the bidi.

Dress: - In the matter of dress, Muslims especially women are greatly influenced by the Meitei sartorial style. Most of the women are attired in a phanek (a kind of sarong indigenously woven and worn by Meitei ladies), with a short kurta over it, the whole (not the lower half of the phanek) covered with an innaphi (shawl made of cotton or silk or a combination) The difference in attire of Muslim women and Meitei women is that the latter wear a short blouse (upto the waist) Above the phanek, Pangals favour a short kurta. The kurtas of older women even reach to the knee. There is also a subtle difference in wearing the phanek. T.C. Hodson wrote: The Pangan (Pangal) women wear Faneks, which they fasten under the right breast, while Meitei women fasten this garment under the left breast. The colours of the faneks of pangan women differ from those used by Manipuris, as for instance, the green used by a Meitei will be darker, less glaring, than the shade of green allowable to the Pangan"[89]. This observation needs to be modified in the light of the new dyes, colours used today in the manufacture of phaneks. These are now fashionable and worn both by Meiteis as well as Pangals. In former times, the phanek was held up securely at the waist by using a 'Khwangnam' (piece of cloth tied around the waist over the phanek). Today, petticoats have replaced the khwang nam. Young Muslim girls are dressed either in frocks or more often in salwar kameez, teenagers follow dictates of fashion and favour Salwar-kameez, handloom made garments have largely given way to factory produced textiles and garments.

The Pangal men also adopted the Meitei khudei (lungi) and are generally seen in this dress, topped either by a shirt or vest. However, the dress common to Muslims Elsewhere in India is gaining popularity not only with the youth but also seniors in the community. Respectable gentlemen, including old men, have taken to wearing kurta /pajama, with an Islamic cap on the head. More adventurous fashionable males don the Sherwani on festive occasions. For daily use, they adhere to the western attire of shirt, trousers, socks and shoes.

On the occasion of marriage too, the Muslim bride largely emulates her Meitei sister, whereas the Pangal bridegroom is attired in white garments (as in Meitei custom) with a turban (kokyet or koyet) or Kashmiri cap worn on the head. Most of the groom's parties are also clad in white. White is the colour of choice in Manipur for all kinds of religious ceremonies.

Pangal women like all other Indian women are fond of jewelry, and adorn themselves with earrings, nose rings – Nasika (which earlier marked out a Muslim women-previously Meiteis never pierced their nose), bangles, necklaces, rings etc. Even very young Muslims sport nose-rings. The more affluent class have ornaments made of gold, the others are content with silver, or now increasingly artificial jewelry. Women used Chank, Mang, Kotbiladar (modern chandroman), Sekra and Binduli for adorning the head and forehead, Karnphul Pipal Patti morbhanwar and bali on the ears.[90]

Language: - After their advent in Manipur, the Muslim who came in 1606 and later, made Manipur their home. They married local Meitei women, and adopted Meiteilon (the language of the Meiteis) as their mother tongue. All Pangals are fluent in the language and use it for all common purposes of life. They are proficient in the subtleties of the language and conversant with proper forms of address. They frequently use Manipuri proverbs, and even compose songs in Manipuri. They enriched Meiteilon with the Turkish, Urdu and Arabic words eg. Rumal-handkerchief, kalam-pen,tandur-bakery,top-canon, kanchi-guard on roof, ain-law, qanoon-law/rule, Anok-spectacle, kameez-shirt, khabar-news, kharif-crop, khali-empty, khum-pot, zeb-pocket, hukum-order, Andaz-quantity, elaka-portion, Amin-person who measures land, Kanoongo-supervisor, kabar-tomb, karbar-business, gulap- rose, darji- tailor, dukan-shop, badnam-defame, badmash-rogue, bazaar-market, shahar-city, hapta-week, etc.[91]

Health: - The age of marriage for a Pangal is earlier than a Meitei. The report on Socio-Economic Survey of Meitei-Pangals states that the means age of marriage for males in uniform throughout the state i.e. 26- 31 years except Chandel district where it is 20.52 only. For women, the mean age of marriage 22.50 years (no child marriage), whereas according to the National Family Health survey, India, 1998-1999, the age of Marriage for males in Manipur in 1999-2000 was 28.6 and for females 25.4 respectively.

The household size of Manipuri Muslims is 6.3, and there is a strong preference for boys. Family planning is not acceptable, as they are not well informed about the new sophisticated tools and techniques, and scientific methods of birth control, and use religion as a pretext. Women from the higher income group bear less children and vice versa for women from the lower income group. In addition, because of early marriage, the years of child bearing are increased. Only thirty-five out of a thousand women access medical services at child birth, government doctors attend only 156 out of 1000 women, nurses attend 342 women out of a thousand. Most women prefer to give birth at home (868 of 1000).

Ailments for less than thirty days are highest in the age group of fifteen to thirty- nine years – 39.59%, it is 36.32% in the age group of zero to fourteen, and only 7.23% in the age group of sixty and above. For ailments extending over thirty days, the most vulnerable group is between forty and fifty nine years (34.87%), 9.44% are in the age group of zero to fourteen years, indicative of parent's interest in the health of their children. Men suffering from ailments are 44.39% and for women it is 55.61% Women are more susceptible to infection disease, because of lack of knowledge, Malnutrition, Anaemia, unbalanced diet etc. Poorer women suffer greatly from poor health. Since most Pangals are disadvantaged economically, when they seek medical attention, it is usually at government hospitals 43.33%. They seem to prefer allopathy in preference to homeopathy and Ayurveda.

With regard to longevity, 38.92% of Muslims die after the age of sixty. Death in the age group of Zero to Fourteen years stands at 29.94%; it is 14.97% for the age group of forty to fifty nine years. Most deaths occur at home perhaps due to lack of access to proper medical health care. Death from natural causes stands at 7.78% Heart failure, Respiratory and central nervous system disorders, fever, jaundice, accident are other leading causes of death.[92]

The percentage of maternal deaths is twelve per thousand. Unwanted pregnancies, where they occur, are a matter of much concern, especially for unwed girls and women. The percent age of women who suffer from malnourishment is 19.03%, and is largely confined to the low income group, most of whom are not literate. The actual percentage however, maybe higher. Women are educated about their bodies; sexual health information is imparted by senior women and female family members. The greatest impediment to good health is the fact that only 5.5% of Muslim women have access to proper sanitation and drinking water.

The figures for HIV + (Rampant in the state) are not available as statistics are not compiled on a community basis. A Lilong woman resident estimated that it amounted to fifteen of one thousand women, or perhaps 1% of 1, 00,000 women. Most affected individuals, especially women do not have access to free or affordable essential drugs including ART, either because they are ignorant of their HIV status, or afraid to access the same because of social stigma. A majority of the Pangals even lack information about over the counter drugs. Women have been increasingly rendered vulnerable to sexually transmitted diseases as also HIV because of partners' irresponsible drug injecting behaviour.

Another factor which adversely impacts women is violence against women. Such incidents are rarely reported, for fear of reprisals, and because the family socializes its members to accept hierarchical gender relations (under Islamic law, the father is the head of the family) Perpetuators of violence are generally known persons. This is exacerbated by unequal division of labour and resources.[94]

References

1. Quazi Hamid Ali-op. cit., p. 25.

2. Khairuddin Choudhury – op.cit., p.11.

3. Mohammad Latif Shah – op.cit., p.196.

4. Thangjam Subhas Singh – op.cit., p. 55.

5. Md. Ahmed Ali Shah – op.cit. p. 61 cit. W.P. Scott – Dictionary of sociology Delhi 1988 p. 221.

6. Ibid., pp. 63-84.

7. Abdus Sahid Chowdary – The Meitei Pangan – Socio-Culture Highlights – Souveniur, 4th Annual Conference of the all Assam Manipuri Muslim students welfare union, Cachar, 1989.

8. Quazi Hamid Ali – op.cit., pp. 26-27.

9. Md. Ahmad Ali Shah – op.cit., p. 86.

10. K.M. Ashraf – Life and conditions of the people of Hindusthan, pp.176.

11. Khairuddin Choudhury op.cit.

12. Thangjam Subhas Singh op.cit. p. 57, cit. Md. Latif Shah – Pangal Manipuri Muslim – People of India, Manipur, Ed. By K.S. Singh Delhi, 1998, p.197.

13. Khairuddin Choudhury – op.cit.

14. Mah Moodah Khaanam, op.cit., pp. 14-15.

15. Kutub Ahmed Mazumdar – 'A Retrospect' – Souvenior op.cit., p. (i).

16. Mahmodah Khaanam, op.cit. p.26 cit. The New Encyclopedia Britanica, p. 332, Vol. 6.

17. Ibid, p. 22, cit J. Roy – History of Manipur (1958) pp.166-167.

18. Salam Irene – Catholic Education in Manipur pp. 58-59 cit. Jamini Devi – Development of Modern system of education in Manipur, and contribution of Sir Johnstone, Souveniour, Johnstone School Centenary celebration 1885-195.

19. Ibid.

20. A. Hakim Shah Khullakpam, op.cit., p.77.

21. Report On Socio- Economic Survey Of Meitei Pangals, op.cit. 41.

22. A. Hakim Shah Khullakpam op.cit., pp.167-168.

23. Mahmoodah Khaanam op.cit. pp. 28-29, cit. M.A. Janab Khan Manipur Muslim pp. 42-45, Shanti press, Congress Bhavan, Imphal, 1972.

24. Salam Irene – Manipur Muslim Women, p. 21 cit. Mahamoodah Khaa Nam, op.cit., pp. 61 and 66.

25. Ibid, p. 20.

26. Report on Socio-Economic Survery op.cit. p. 41.

27. Salam Irene – op.cit. p. 21 cit. Board of Secondary Eduaction in Manipur 1981.

28. Ibid – p. 22.

29. Ibid.

30. Ibid p.23 cit. Syed Ahmed – Status of Muslim women in Manipur pp. 58-59.

31. Laljian Begum – Muslim women's Educational status in Manipur – pp. 1, 2 and 4.

32. Salam Irene op.cit., p. 25.

33. Ibid pp. 25-26. Cit Report op.cit., pp. 47-49 .

34. Ibid cit. Mahmoodah Khaanam op.cit., p .87.

35. Quazi Hamid Ali op.cit, p. 29.

36. Md. Latif Shah – op.cit., p.197.

37. Tingneichong Gangte – Women's Role in the Twentieth Century Manipur A historical study, unpublished Ph.D. Thesis, Manipur University 2008 p .67, cit. S.Q.R. Ilyas (ed) Sim News Bulletin, Vol.5, No. 5 + 6, Aligarh, 1982, p. 21.

38. Md. Ahmed Ali Shah, op.cit. p.42, cit. Khonthang vol.1, No.1, Aug. 1978, pp. 5-6.

39. Report on socio Economic Survey of Meitei – Pangal, op.cit. p. 26.

40. Sheikh Amir Ayub Shishti – Polygamy and Islam, The Sangai Express – 2-8-09.

41. Tingneichong op.cit. P.68 cit S.Q.R. Ilyas op.cit. p. 21.

42. Md. Ahmed Ali Shah op.cit., pp. 45-46.

43. Md. LAtif Shah op.cit., p.196.

44. Tingneichong Gangte – op.cit., pp. 71-72.

M.A. Rahman – The Culture of Manipur Muslims (Pangals) p. 43.

46. Thangham Subhas Singh op.cit,. p.75 cit. Kheiruddin Khullakpam – Turko Afghanchada Naoda Circles, Lilong, Manipur 1997, p. 210.

47. Ibid p.76 cit. M.A. Janab Khan op.cit., p. 35.

48. Md. Latif Shah op.cit., p.197.

49. Quazi Hamid Ali – op.cit., p. 30.

50. Md. Latif Shah, op.cit., p.197.

51. Ricahrd M.Eaton op.cit. p. 279 cit. the glorious Koran: A bilingual Edition with English translation introduction and notes, trans. Marmaduke Pickthall (London; George Allen and Unwin 1976) Sura 4; 34.

52. Salam Irene op.cit. p.13.

53. Syed Ahmed – Women Employment and Development: A case study of Manipuri Muslim women, p.10- Souveniour – 2 day state level seminar – women empowerment and development with special reference to Manipur, March 2009.

54. Salam Irene, op.cit. p.13.

55. Md Riyaz Ahmed Shah – Status of Muslim women in Manipur state, pp. 3-4.

56. Salam Irene op.cit., pp.13-14, cit. Richard M. Eaton, op.cit. pp. 298-299.

57. Constantine R: Manipur, Maid of the Mountains, Lancer publishers, 1981, New Delhi, p. 46.

58. MD. Riyaz Ahmed Shah – op.cit.

59. Salam Irene. Op.cit,. p.16.

60. Asgahar Ali Engineer – Islam and liberation theology – Rights of women under Islam, Sterling Publishers Pvt. Ltd., p.175.

61. Mh. Ahmed Ali Shah, op.cit. pp. 57-59.

62. Manu Bhaskar -Family Law and customary practices of Muslims – The eastern Anthropologist, Vol. 49, No.1. pp. 13-14.

63. K. Kunjani Devi – Muslim women's status in the family and society in Manipur p. 3.

64. Lucy Carroll – The Pakistani Talaq in Enlgish Law, T. Mahmood(ed,) Islamic and Comparative Law quarterly Vol. II, No. 1, 1982, pp. 17-18.

65. Md. Ahmad Ali Shah op.cit. p.51.

66. Manu Bhaskar – op.cit., p.12.

67. Ram Prasad Khosla – Mughal Kingship and Nobillity p.1

68. Md. Latif Shah op.cit., p.195.

69. Md. Riyazuddin Chaudhury – Muslim contribution to the culture of Manipur p.42, Souvenior – Manipur Sahitya Parishad golden Jubilee.

70. N. Devendra Singh – Identities of Migrated people in Manipur, published by centre for Manipur studies, Manipur University 1994, pp. 24-29.

71. Md. Riyazuddin Chaudhury. Op.cit – cit. Ningthourol Lampupa, p.103, Mcculloch – An account of the valley of Manipur, p.15, Higgins – List of clans of the Manipuri Muhammadans, Nongshup Haram, Nongsamei.

72. Thangjam Subhas Singh op.cit, pp. 40-41 cit. B. Kullachandra and Badaruddin, op.cit., pp. 33-34, 102-103.

73. Quazi Hamid Ali – op.cit., pp. 25-26.

74. Thangjam Subhas Singh op.cit., pp.48-49, cit. B. Kullachandra and Badar uddin, pp. 82-83.

75. N. Devendra Singh op.cit., pp. 2 9-30.

76. Md. Riyazuddin Chaudhury, op.cit.

77. W. Ibohal Singh, op.cit.

78. Mahamoodah Khaanam, op.cit. pp. 7-9.

79. Quazi Hamid Ali, op.cit., p. 29.

80. N. Devendra Singh op.cit., pp. 29.

81. Thangjam Subhas Singh, op.cit. pp. 129-133 cit. B. Kullachandra and Badar uddin Meitei Pangals Hourakpham, Imphal 1991, pp. 3, 78.

82. Report on socio-economic survey of Meitei Pangals, op.cit. pp. 64-86.

83. J.B. Gangoly – An Economic History of North East India, 1826 – 1947, pp. 294-295.

84. Thangjam Subhas Singh op.cit. pp. 67-70.

85. Report on socio-economic survey of Meitei Pangals, op.cit. pp. 85-86.

86. Thangjam Subhas Singh op.cit., p. 66 cit. B. Kullachandra Sharma

87. Md. Latif Shah, op.cit, p.195.

88. Md. Ahmad Ali Shah, op.cit., pp.73-75.

89. Thangjam Subhas Singh, op.cit., p. 66.

90. T.C. Hodson – The Meitheis, Delhi, 1975, p.18.

91. N. Wontharla – The social and cultural life of Muslims in Manipur – Unpublished M.phil dissertation, Manipur University 2008, p. 39.

92. A. Hakim Shah Khullakpam, op.cit., pp.168-169.

93. Report on socio-economic survey of Meitei Pangals, op.cit. pp. 54-63.

94. Salam Irene, op.cit. pp. 15-17.

3

Role of Muslims in The Economy

The state has an agrarian based economy. The Muslims who made Manipur their home from 1606 onwards, preferred to establish their settlements by the side of water bodies, like rivers, lakes, canals, tanks. The reason for this preference was their ability to grow pulses, grain, vegetables, and herbs on this fertile land. Prior to the advent of colonial rule in Manipur (1891), Manipur had a self-sufficient economy but all this changed under the British, and the Nupilan (women's war) of 1939 was fought to prevent the export of rice from Manipur, at a time when people had no Rice to meet their daily requirement of food.

After Manipur's merger with the Indian Union in 1949, the state began to grow increasingly dependent on imports of all essential items, including Rice-the staple grain, pulses, oil, salt, sugar etc. But the Ingkholsangba of the Pangal community continued to cultivate the land, as a source of sustenance; moreover, more than half of the Meitei-Pangal possess cultivated land, and live in villages, adjacent to these lands.

The socio- economic setting of the Muslims in the state is strikingly rural-based who still subsist on the age-old Agro-oriented pursuits. Agriculture is the mainstay of almost eighty percent of the Muslims in the State. Merely, 2.27% of the Muslims are in the government sector, while the remaining population is engaged in various categories of low profile, informal or unorganised economic activities like hotel-industry, rickshaw-pulling, repairing and assembling of cycles, tricycles, and motor vehicles, etc.[1]

The Pangals possess great skill in agriculture-everything they planted sprouted, and grew in profusion. They can be said to have 'green fingers'. But of land in Manipur, R. Brown writes'. "The whole land system of the valley starts with the assumption that all the land belongs to the Raja, and is his to give away, or retain as he pleases.[2] Khagemba's reign was marked by great agricultural development. The King himself was a great patron of agriculture. But in the seventeenth century, the valley of Manipur was a swampy area, which required constant draining of water from the marshes to the river systems. Khagemba took interest in providing irrigation facilities to the people. Rivers and streams were dredged, canals were dug, like Kyang Kong, Takhen khong etc. Bunds were constructed to control the flood from the rivers. These measures benefitted the Pangal cultivators, enabling them to increase production. A further spurt was given, when agricultural technology was improved, with the introduction of transplanting system 'Lingba' of paddy cultivation, introduced by Muslim peasants who were war captives. These Muslim peasants introduced the plough drawn by the bullock and buffalo.[3] Despite Brown's assertion, Md. Latif Shah states that ownership of land was on an individual basis, some of the Pangal are land less, and live with their relatives.[4] But prior to 1891, the Manipur valley was traditionally divided into two categories viz. Ingkhol (homestead land) and Lou (cultivable/ agricultural land). Among the latter category, was one known as 'Pangal Lou; this land was given by the king to deserving persons who had displayed valour in war, hunt and so on.[5] Unlike the Manalou (Also given to persons other than Pangals for distinguished service), after the death of the original grantee, the land could be retained by his heirs/ family. In 1891, there were about 200 persons holding this land.

The revenue system was systematized with the improvement of agricultural production- the cultivators were to pay revenue in form of paddy to the state. The land was now owned by the king in theory, but the nobles had utilized them by employing peasants, who were possessors of these lands, and payers of rent to the state.[6] Many Muslims were given Sageis because of their skill in cultivation eg. Hawai- ingkhol Mayum (Bean, garden, house), The Muslims opened an exclusive garden viz Ningthem Ingkhol at Khomidok Heịnou Khongnembi, on receipt of a royal order, directing them to grow fruits and vegetables there.[7]

The Muslims were liable to render lallup to the state. Each individual who performed lallup was entitled to cultivate for his support, one pari of land, equivalent to about three English acres, subject to the regular payment of tax in kind.[8] People were also given the right to reclaim new land, for cultivation. Anybody who wanted to reclaim new land should first take the permission of the king. And the land so granted could be cultivated the first one year, free of tax. The tenant possessed a rightful claim to the reclaimed land, and the king could not dispossess him without sufficient compensation. The tenant could lend or even sell the land. But after three years, he had to pay tax in kind at the rate fixed by the state.[9]

Even though the large majority of Pangals are engaged in cultivation, out of the total Meitei-Pangal population engaged in economic activity, a recent study cities that only 40.27% are engaged in agriculture, even though cultivation does not yield much income.[10] The Muslims had originally come from Bengal, and according to Dun, the mode of cultivation of the soil in Manipur does not differ from the practice in Bengal, so far as tillage is concerned. In Manipur, the operation of scratching up the soil, and preparing the field for reception of the rice seed, commences in February, and in May they sow, what is called 'pung-hul' or dry seed, cast in dry ground. In June, the rains having set in, the field is brought by successive ploughings and harrowing, into a state of liquid mud, and in this, the pung-hul is cast. The seed for the punghul is first quickened, by being moistened with water, and kept in a covered basket until it shoots. As this seed floats on the surface of the mud, it has to be carefully watched until it takes root, and three or four leaves spring up, in order to protect it from wild ducks and other birds. After this comes the 'lingba' or transplanting the seed for the plants which are destined to be transplanted are usually sown very close in plots, carefully prepared for the purpose. When the transplanting season arrives, the plants are pulled in handfuls out of the ground. The roots are by washing, divested of all the earth attached to them, and having been taken to the field, they are, one by one, separately inserted in the mud for a time after transplanting; they look as if they were all withered up, but they soon spring up and afford an excellent crop. If the ground has been carefully deprived of weeds before sowing the crops, weeding after wards is not required. The only cultivation of any importance is that of rice; not a particle of manure is ever placed on the ground, and yet, year after year, good crops are raised on the same spot. The yield has of course lessened from what it was, but its being still so considerable, as it evinces a very rich soil. The mainstay however of Manipur, is the crop raised at Thoubal (where many Pangals reside), and its vicinity. There the river, once at least in the year, inundates the rice-fields, giving them amazing fertility. About Thoubal, they weed with a harrow, which drawn by a buffalo over the rice-fields, uproots indiscriminately weeds and rice. The former die and the rice-plants take root again, and are not injured. When the rice begins to ripen, it has to be watched against the depredations of immense flights of birds. Deer and other wild animals also do a great deal of mischief, and against them, precautions have to be taken. The rice having ripened, is cut with a knife (thangol), slightly curved at the top, and having a rough edge like a saw. As it is cut, it is laid in handfuls on the ground, and when dry, tied in sheaves. These sheaves are carried to the part of the field most convenient for the purpose, and the rice beat from them on a large reed mat. After having been winnowed by means of fans, the rice is ready for the granary and removed to it. The sun-dried rice keeps very well in husk, but when cleared of the husks, it can be kept for a short time only. The straw is left lying in a pile round the place where the paddy was beat out. Except as fuel, no use is made of it. It will be seen from the above description, that the mode of cultivation, the planting and transplanting of rice, etc., is the same as that followed in eastern Bengal. The fertility of the soil, which continues without Manure to yield good crops, is doubtless owing to the fact that the rivers flowing through the valley, are in the rainy season, enormously loaded with mud, which becomes annually deposited in the rice-fields, the soil of the valley is nearly all throughout of excellent quality, and of great depth.[11]

During the reign of Chandrakirti Maharaj, the Muslims after getting permission of the king dug a river in Lilong in 1880. This diverted river, from the Imphal River at Lilong proper, returned to it at Iramsiphai. Its length is about seven kilometers, breadth- fifty metres, and depth-fifteen metres. The river diverts excess water from Imphal River, and provides it for agricultural purposes, irrigating the fields on both sides of the river.[12]

About the varieties and mode of rice cultivation, J.B. Ganguly observes; "About nineteen varieties of rice were cultivated; a few of which were early varieties, yields of which were much higher, took about six months to be ready for harvest. Cultivators grew much more of the late varieties than the early ones. There were at least fifteen late varieties raised in Manipur.

Cultivation of late varieties followed the method of transplantation.[13]

Paddy grown in Manipur is divided into Anganphou (early) and Athengphou (late) crop. Saji khong, Tumai, Kabow phou, Phourel-Anganba are the favourite varieties among the early crop. Among the late-growing variety, Phourel, Luining and Yenthik are popular. Farmers' preference ran for the early variety, as it involved less time and labour. The other late varieties were Moirang phou, phowkok chahow, chahow masa palbi, phoungang, Touthabi, Chahow Poireoton, Chahow Munkhang, Kakcheng phou, Haitup phou. Sagol Yangba, Chahow Erikole and Chahow Sempak.

Of rice which formed the staple diet, Braudel has compared rice cultivation to wheat cultivation. The advantages that accrue from the former are first, that unhusked rice can be stored for a longer period; it is less susceptible to attacks of malaria, because in the plains, rice fields are irrigated by muddy water of the rivers carrying silt. The fertility of the rice fields is restored, and mosquitoes avoid muddy water. Moreover, valley growers usually raised two or sometimes even three crops of rice every year. Or instead of rice, some other crops, such as wheat, barley, vegetables, beans, pulses, could be harvested as the second or third crop between two rice-crops. "The rice field is thus a factory" observes Braudel.[14]

The great advantage of rice lies in the possibility of a second harvest of it, from the same field, and so a large and densely settled population could thrive. Certainly rice productions in valleys could provide a degree of security of food supply to the growers. This accounted for the demographic growth in the rice growing region such as Manipur. The Meitei Pangal lives in the rice bowl of the valley.

Besides rice, the Meitei Pangals grew some jute and also opium. In the homestead, they cultivated onion, garlic, ginger, spices like jeera (cumin) and methi, tobacco, mustard plant, kumchak, palak, hawai mangal (dal), HawaiAmubi(a kind of bean), hawai mangal Machin Mubi(dal), Sagol Hawai, Morok (chilli),Yaingang (turmeric), khongdrum (bottle guord), mariel (pumpkin), pangal khamen (brinjal), tejpata, tomato, potato, cabbage caulli flower, lady's finger, swu (raw material of paper), radish, turnip. Pangal and Kei khongta Ingkhol were popular for production of vegetables and cereals. Some cereals were grown in limited quantity- kasari, chana, mairongbi- hawai, chak hawai, nunghuwai. In their ingkhols, they planted fruit trees- mango (heinou khongnembi and Meitei heinou), lemon, jack fruit, guava, plum, cherry, and peach.[15]

Besides the bullock or buffalo, agricultural implements used in rice cultivation were the 'kangpot' – a kind of sledge drawn by buffalo, the 'langol' or plough, the 'ukaianalba' or smooth harrow, the phao-intok or wooden paddy spoon, the humai or fan used for winnowing, the ukai samjet or toothed harrow, the cheirong or paddy thresher, the thangol or sickle, the yot or spade, the thangchao or large dao and yeinaphak or threshing mat.[16]

As highlighted by Braudel, (Civilization and capitalism 15th-16th centuries, Vol.1, p. 24) culture of rice growing in the plains influences the socio-political and economic life and institutions of the people concerned. Rice cultivation involves 'enormous concentration on work', through mobilization of 'human capital', and erection and management of irrigation system, under the supervision of some dominant superior authority. This would not be possible without a 'stable society and state authority'. Extension of rice cultivation into new areas has to be in an orderly manner which calls for state control. Rich growing villages formed into clusters, in order to deal with the collective requirements of irrigation, and to ensure security of life and property, including the rice crop. Braudel's survey revealed that successful operation of rice fields was associated with high population and strict social discipline. The Meiteis (including Meitei-Pangal), manifested such social discipline and supervisory state authority.[17]

In the post-war period (World War II), the state was facing food scarcity. One of the Pangals launched a 'grow more food' campaign. This was Qazi Mohammad Waliallah, the first arts graduate among the Pangals. He had been the Secretary of the State paddy collection committee during the war against the Japanese at Imphal. The king had inadequate stocks to supply his troops with food. The secretary busied himself procuring paddy on a loan basis, to supply the necessary ration to the army, who were in dire straits. The 'grow more food' campaign was launched in 1950. Different types of high-yielding seeds were distributed, effecting a revolutionary change in the Rabi harvest. The officers employed, conducted extensive tours, sensitizing cultivators about the benefits, and also teaching them how to guard their crops against pests.[18] The

Government of Manipur introduced the patta in writing on 24th oct. 1891. Its tax was severalty. Tax on ordinary people was Rs 1 |- per pari. The Meitei Pangals paid the tax.[19]

Fishery- Fish trade was a component of Manipur's economy. The Ngarunghanba was in charge of the fishery department Shellungbas assisted, while the Pukhranba with the help of Ngarunghanba supplied the Lalmies (soldiers) with fish. Meitei Pangals could fish from adjacent lakes, but were barred from fishing in lakes given to favourites by the king. The Qazi-Pat near Kyamgei was a lake, granted to Tolen Qazi Ipham (Barkootodah) for his lifetime, by King Gambhir Singh as a reward for his active service in the Anglo Burmese war (1824-1826). The Waithou-pat, Poirou-pat, Kharung-pat, Ikop-pat, Guru-pat, Pumlen-pat, Nganglou were important lakes for purposes of fishing.[20]

Seventy percent of Muslims are fish farmers- they mainly rear Rou, Silver carp, grass carp and common carp in their ponds. The cost of a fingerling ranges from fifty paise to Rs. Five. The fish feed on a special grass known as hoop; silver carp eat insects, whereas Rou feeds on the excreta of grass and silver carp. Fingerlings are bought in the monsoons, and are ready for sale within ten to twelve months. The price of fish differs according to the variety, silver and grass carp are not expensive, but Rou and other varieties of carp, can fetch a handsome price. The larger the fish, the higher the cost. A space of two acres is required for rearing 10,000 Fishes. Mud walls are built on the sides of the ponds, but in times of floods fish are swept away and the farmer faces a loss. But in good seasons, he could earn double the amount of the initial investment. The returns from pissiculture are uncertain, so Muslims do not depend only on fish farming.[21]

The Muslim however are adept in fishing, especially as fish supplemented the staple rice in their diet. Proximity to water sources, facilitated procurement of this supplement, and like the Meitei's, the Pangals are fond of partaking of fish. Some of them even sell the dry, fermented Fish, relished by the inhabitants of the state.

The government, recognising the importance of fish farming as an item of diet, and a source of financial income, provides loans to farmers, and assists them in various ways. Two fish breeding, centres have been set up at Wangoi in Thoubal, and in Lamphelpat in Imphal west. The rivers and lakes in addition, provided a good network of communication by using small canoes called 'hee' and rafts called 'Pong'. These were important in Manipur, before the coming of the British, as there was no road.[22]

Poultry farming- Many of the Muslims earn their livelihood by rearing of chickens, ducks and geese, but the chicken coops are rudimentary wire mesh enclosures, which have an aluminum channel filled with grain running alongside the poultry coops. Although cleanliness and hygiene are essential for running a poultry farm-A strong unpleasant smell normally emanates from the poultry enclosures. Poultry farmers are able to earn a healthy profit, as chicken meat in particular is greatly relished especially by the youth. Earlier, Meiteis did not partake of it, but both chicken and duck meat have gained popularity in the community;

A large section of elders and orthodox individuals continue to shun it. Despite endemic bandhs, general strikes, economic blockades on the highways, which adversely impact livelihood, prices of poultry meat exhibit an upward mobility, and customers continue to buy meat at inflated prices, as they greatly Relish poultry dishes. Inflated prices are also associated with the sale of eggs, especially in times of scarcity or strife, which occurs with frequent regularity. Most people relish eggs, not just for break fast, but also as a mid day or evening snack (egg pakoras or plain boiled eggs).

The benefits of this kind of business extend to both the semi-urban and rural economy. It enables people who have no land asset, to earn a healthy income: moreover, it provides a nutritious diet to people in both urban and rural areas. As most Pangals reside in rural areas, it is possible and eminently viable for them to set up small, medium or large poultry farms with a minimum capital investment. The poultry farmers take due care to inoculate the birds against all forms of disease. For instance, the farmers suffered great financial loss for no fault of their own, during the recent worldwide bird-flu epidemic. Broiler birds are easy to rear, in two to three months, the chicks grow into healthy birds, which are sold for a profit in different markets scattered all over the state, especially the Imphal valley. Local varieties of duck and chicken are the dish of choice, and are sold at high prices, as the meat is greatly relished by the populace. Geese are also reared, but have not attained the popularity of chicken and duck, as an essential part of one's diet. Poultry is sold by weight; both live birds and dressed poultry are easily procurable, depending on individual preference.

Farm eggs are much in demand-they sell for much more than the eggs imported into Manipur from other States in the country. The great advantage of poultry farming is not merely financial gain, but that it provides an essential nutrient or supplement to daily intake of food.

Poultry sheds are made of bamboo and wood, with a bamboo chatai (mat) mixed with straw and mud on the floor. Iron bars or 'chali' are used for walling. Upto a height of one and a half feet, above the ground, the shed is made of brick, mud and straw. The poultry sheds have openings for cross ventilation; the roofing comprises aluminium sheets, high at the centre top, tapering down to the sides. This design facilitates the entry of both light and air. The average requirement of a bird is two square feet from birth upto a period of forty days, there after four feet is required. Poultry farming has the added advantage of enriching the soil, forty laying hens produce one ton of poultry manure annually. The expenditure of feed for poultry can be partly offset, by the increase in crop yield (from the homesteads or cultivable land), resulting from an application of poultry manure.[23]

Poultry farming, except in time of epidemics, assures a fixed or at least a fluctuating income. Farms are usually run on an individual basis; the farmer is assisted in his chores by family members; all together supervise and manage the entire operation, from rearing poultry, to sale of both meat and eggs. Poultry farms are usually situated adjacent to the homestead; supervision is thus made easy, especially as poultry are kept in a confined space.

Cattle Rearing- Not only were Muslims partial to meat, but they were proficient in rearing cattle to meet their own requirements for milk and food. And for sale in adjoining villages and towns. In the past, they had gifted the King (Khagemba) with sweetmeats made of milk. But over a period of time, a more recent group of settlers' viz. members of the Nepali community have practically monopolized the rearing of cattle for purposes of milk supply. But as late as 1891, cattle were, imported through Manipur from Burma, and exported to Cachar, mainly Burmese buffaloes. Many Manipuri traders including Meitei-Pangals were engaged in this trade.[24] Nevertheless, the Muslims have not been able to introduce mechanised, modern dairy farms in the state.

Iron Tools Manufacture – Knowledge of gun-making came to Manipur along with the Muslims. According to Janab khan, during the reign of king Mungyamba (1562-1592) three gun-making Muslims were allowed to settle in Manipur.[25] In order to make guns, the Muslims would have had to be conversant with iron manufacture. Iron ore was found in Manipur in the form of titaniferous oxydulated ore, in the beds of small streams, south of Thoubal, and in hills near Lengatel. Pemberton in his report of 1839 cites that the Manipur had developed indigenous technology to locate iron ore deposits in the hills and river beds, and to smelt iron from ore, and manufactured a number of tools and implements. It was easy to discover the whereabouts of iron deposits in the hills, as grasses covering them, almost invariably looked withered, an indication of their existence. For hitting the iron ore deposits in river beds, a unique technique was used. At the end of the rainy season, when the river-bed became silt less, a skilled workman thrust his iron spear into the ground, and lifting it out of the bed, checked if the iron spear head had any small particles of iron ore adhering to it. The iron spear head, in order to attract iron, needs to have a magnetic property. When not in use, it was vertically inserted in the ground of the court yard. According to Pemberton's estimate, the proportion of recovery of iron from ore, through the smelting process amounted to fifty percent, which was quite satisfactory. The iron works were run mainly in three villages under Boodhee Rajah. Axes, hoes, spears, arrow heads, long iron blades used as 'dao' with wooden handle were produced.[26] The Muslims being mainly cultivators used all these implements for defence too (against marauding raids of tribes). It is possible that they were associated with its manufacture, as iron was mainly found at Thoubal (a dominant Muslim habitation).

The process of forging iron was done in a rough shed, constructed for the purpose. In the shed, two hollow wooden cylinders, in which pistons Fringed with feathers were worked up and down. The lower ends of cylinders were buried in the ground, side by side, and from them two bamboo tubes converged just below; the charcoal fire was placed in front of this stone, and when the pistons overworked, a very strong draught is obtained. The blacksmith produced simple, agricultural implements.[27]

Pottery: - Manipuri potters possessed great skill and produced cooking and other utensils, using metals, such as brass, copper, bell-metal, clay, and even stone. Various pots, such as cooking pots and water pitchers were made of clay. Even sand stone was used to make eating bowls, which were artificially blackened. Such stone pots were beautifully polished.[28] As early as the reign of King Khagemba, when the first Muslims came and settled in Manipur, one of them, A sepoy named Nuriya Shaikh, had presented an exquisite mud-pot to the king. In recognition of the potter's skill his clan had been named 'Phusam'. Even today, Muslims continue to produce good quality stone pots, especially at Thoubal, but these are no longer popular in middle and upper class households, where ceramic, glass, plastic, meloware, non-stick aluminiums pans have pride of place, and for a Muslim potter it is difficult to eke out a sustainable livelihood. But the wheel-making techniques of the Muslims can be upgraded, to experiment with alternative mediums, other than stone, as for example ceramic. With the skill inherited through generation Muslim potters using the wheeling technique, can produce exquisite products, if they receive the necessary training.

The pots used traditionally for storing clean water in a house are known as 'Sanabun'. Muslims are credited with introducing the style of pot-punkangnanbi, which later came to be termed the 'Sanabun'.[29] The importance of a sanabun is underlined by the fact that it forms part of the 'a wonpot' of the Manipuri bride.

Professional Workers– Manipur artisans acquired skills in different disciplines. Their professional skills as carpenters were highly prized in Cachar and Sylhet. The entire Manipur landscape in the valley is dotted with carpentry works. Brown has observed that the good Manipuri carpenters were capable of turning out 'First – Rate works', and could 'imitate English work successfully. Manipuri turners produced artistic wood carvings and articles of ivory. They could also produce articles of silver and glass, and knew the art of electroplating.[30] The Muslims right from the time of their settlement, had been adept in the use of the 'phundrei' (wooden lathe), for fine polishing of wood. This is why the Muslim Phundrei clan was entrusted with manufacturing hookak stands and necks, and the top of canopies – paygimaton.[31]

'Topo', a machine for pressing sugarcane was also introduced by the Muslims.[32] Brown stated that Manipuri artisans could make good serviceable locks, and could at a pinch, repair and clean a clock. James Johnstone has also noted the high calibre of Manipuri artisans, who were patronized by the kings in their pursuit` of mechanical arts. He –"Maharaja Chandrakirti Singh, had a great taste for mechanical arts of all kinds and a vast fund of information which he had acquired by questioning." But the colonial writers do not differentiate between Meitei and Meitei-Pangal artisans; however, it is certain, that some of these artisans were almost exclusively employed for the production of articles to meet the royal court's demand. (Some what akin to the 'karkhanas' of the Delhi sultanate) In fact, many of then worked in the palace workshop, where articles were fabricated in accordance with the Rajah's instructions. It was a system of monopolistic demand of the king, for the services of the most skilled workers, of the different professional groups. Such groups constituted exclusive caste-like formations. Because of this exclusiveness, number of such skilled artisans remained very limited, and so also the quantum of their outputs.[33]

Since the Muslims were given Sageis after the occupation they pursued, they must have formed part of the skilled group of artisans, especially, as since their settlement, many Muslims were assigned duties in / near, the palace. They had at the very outset, presented a beautiful palanquin to the king Khagemba and, although the art of making paper in Manipur had been acquired from Chinese; 'the Meiteis learnt the technology of the typology of the Chinese hand-made paper making tradition.[34] The Muslim migrants advanced the technique which they had learnt in Bengal, before they came to Manipur. The Chesam clan is credited with introducing the art of manufacturing paper. The indigenous writing material in Manipur was Agar bark.[35] It was a fact that Seikh Chunait was a skilled person who made paper during king Khagemba's rule. Some Urdu and Sylheti Bengali words were also introduced into the Archaic Meitei script, e.g., 'Bangal' as 'Pangal', 'Basa', as 'Pasa', 'Mughal', as 'Mangkan', 'Pathan', as 'Fancha'.[36] The state in the pre-colonial period, followed a policy of protecting and patronizing Manipur's cottage industries. The government levied custom duties on all articles imported into the state, and also on a few articles exported out of Manipur.

In the mid-nineteenth century, Imphal grew into an urban area. Its population in 1881 was 60,000 people living in Imphal, besides the king and his nobles and their families, depended on the supplies of many goods produced in the rural areas. In some spheres, labour specialisation in the production process of goods emerged. Some groups of producers produced exclusively nonfarm items of goods. As a result, the process of exchanging goods for goods, in some cases, (barter), and of exchanging goods for money in certain other cases, evolved in Manipur's economy. Transaction of goods took place in the markets spread over different parts of the valley. The markets places were in the open, or in shop-houses, built in the market.[37] In all markets, Muslim traders were evident; at the peripheries the men sold poultry, as only women had access to the market plots as sellers and as buyers.

Some Meitei Pangals were employed as 'Mahuts' and elephant hunters, and also to procure ivory for the government. The government of Manipur maintained relations in respect of the elephant trade, with the elephant kheda of the Cacharis. In the nineteenth century, the value of an elephant was Rs. 300/-. Elephants were used for hiding battle swords and shields, its bones for sword handles, and ivory for commerce.[38] After the war of 1824-26, some Cachari Muslims came to Manipur to pursue trade between Cachar and Manipur. Among them, one Parumiya (Farukh Mia) Choudhury became a prominent trader in Manipur. Because of his trading activities, Parumiya Choudhury was rewarded with royal gifts by King Nara Singh in February, 1845.[39]

In the 2001 population census, the percentage share of Muslim workers to the total state workers was found to be 7.42% only. Further, the number of Muslim workers to the total Muslim population was recorded at 36.75%, while out of the total population of Manipur the percentage of workers was 43.62% at the state level. The majority of the Pangals work in household enterprises as own account worker (self-employed person who operates own enterprise on their own account, or with one or a few partners, usually without hiring any labour. The person may have unpaid helpers to assist). The districts of Imphal West, Bishnupur, Thoubal and Chandel recorded 9% above the state average of 48.97%. Again, amongst the male workers at the state level, 50.25% worked as own account workers, while 21.39% worked as regular, salaried/ wage employees.

Economic Contribution and Women's Role in Development

The women of North East India were free from the handicaps of the purdah system (including the Meitei Pangals). They enjoyed freedom both inside and outside their homes. (Women from upper class families may have been more restricted in movement outside the home). The environment was conducive to their actual participation in the different sectors of productive activity. They played an active role in agricultural operations, animal husbandry, collection of Forest produce, and running of household industries, like spinning and weaving of cotton, silk and woolen textiles, and preparing cloths, besides managing house keeping. The people of both the plains and hills of North East India, had predominantly subsistence Economies, based mainly on cultivation of food and non food crops, partly by practicing the system of settled cultivation in the plains and partly by that of swidden (Shifting) cultivation in the hills. The agrarian sector also covered collection of forest produce, hunting, Fishing and animal husbandry, of course, this primary economic sector could not be sustained without having the secondary sector, consisting of household industries, to produce necessaries like cotton, woolen and silk clothes, and to process agricultural crops, forest products, dairy and poultry products, etc. The region also had some surplus over subsistence for disposal, of which the people carried out some volume of trade and exchange (mostly of barter type), both internal and external. In this paradigm of economic activities, the woman's role was of vital importance, since they were involved in productive activities in all the three sectors of the economy. Many women, particularly of Manipur, took part in trading activities with much acumen that helped boost total volume of productive activities and family incomes.

In fact, women constituted nearly 50% (if not more) of the total effective strength of the economy's labour force. While the men folk were frequently required to render military service to the state, their participation in agriculture and allied activities on a sustained basis was minimal. Had the women not regularly participated in farming and non-farming activities these economics would not have endured. Given the extreme low level of capital accumulation, if at all there was any, capital output ratio was nearly nil. Given also the fact that technology of production was of a very low level, labour-out put ratio contrast,was very high. And in this situation the women labour power played the most crucial role in keeping the economic system going.[40]

The economic condition of the Meitei Pangal during the years following their initial settlement was believed to be good. The community enjoyed the respect of the state Ruler and subjects alike, because they were brave, honest and hard working. But over a period of time, their economic condition worsened, compelling women, and even children to work, in order to eke out a livelihood.[41] Women contributed to the family income by participating in the labour force; simultaneously they presided over household management.

According to distribution of persons by principal usual activity status, it has been found, that as many as 90.12% of the females are outside the labour force. This does not mean that a mere ten percent of Muslim women work- on the contrary, majority of the Muslim women are absorbed in the pursuit of the sustainable livelihood. But they are outside the umbrella of an organized, recognized labour force. One of the main reasons for the official statistic could be illiteracy; however, there exists the possibility of concealing the reality, due to prestige, simultaneously, bias cannot be ruled out. As per the results of the 55th round 1999 – 2000 of NSS, the percentage of females in rural areas of Manipur was estimated at 15.3 amongst the persons usually employed in principal status, against the all India average of 23.1%. In the sample survey it was found to be 14.2% for Manipur and 11.7% for all India in the urban areas. In the 2001 census, out of the total Muslim workers, 60.29% were male workers, while 39.71% were female workers. The same trend was observed at the state level too, except for the fact that the difference is marginal with the male and female workers recorded at 55.78% and 44.22% respectively in the 2001 census. The male-female work participation ratio may also be examined by confining only to the subset of population, usually employed in the principal status.

Percentage of persons Employed in Activity by Sex and district of Manipur 2004.

District	*Male*	*Female*	*Person*
Imphal East	87.41	12.59	100.00
Imphal West	82.43	17.57	100.00
Bishnupur	83.02	16.98	100.00
Thoubal	85.09	14..91	100.00
Churachandpur	76.00	24.00	100.00
Chandel	90.67	9.33	100.00
Manipur	85.46	14.54	100.00

It is apparent that male employment is significantly higher than female employment, and female work participation rate is highest in Churachandpur. But it is important to be cognizant of the fact that Muslim women are pursuing what is labeled non economic activities, which nevertheless result in economic gain, for instance maintenance of kitchen gardens, household poultry rearing, free collection of fish, free collection of fire wood, grinding of food grains, cooking, washing, serving, collection of water etc. If these non-economic activities are converted to economic value, and if these are counted the work participation ratio for females would be considerably higher.[42]

All Manipuri women inclusive of the Pangals are industrious by nature, and besides all the above mentioned activities, they work in agriculture and other income generating activities. It is an age – old tradition for women in the region to shoulder all the internal trade of the state. At Imphal, there is a large all women's market in the heart of the city, believed to have been founded by king Khagemba (1597-1652), known as Khwairamband Bazar or Ima Keithel, where over two thousand women occupy stalls. The entire market is managed by women. Markets such as this, but of smaller size, are found in every nook and corner of the state. As a matter of fact, the work participation rate of women in Manipur is generally higher than the corresponding all India, female work participation rate. The state reports the highest proportion of women, 20%, engaged in household industry, of all the Indian states, as against the national average of 5%. The female work participation rate of the state according to the 1981 census was 2, 08,602 in rural areas and 7, 45,451 for urban areas.[43]

Economic activities are usually distributed according to age; for example, less arduous tasks or responsibilities are assigned to 'machanupi' (small girls), different works to the 'laishabi' (young, unmarried girls, 'mous' (wives) and 'hanubis' older ladies. But there is no hard and fast distinction, and there is a cross-over of tasks.[44]

What sets the Manipuri women apart in the economic sphere is its unique historical experience. The old adage; a man who does not go to the loisang (office), and a woman who does not go to the keithel (market), both are worthless, and the fruit of knowledge is from fathers and grandfathers, the reserved wealth is from mothers and grandmothers, underlines the economic importance of women.[45] A Muslim woman can have a delinquent husband punished, if he is fit and capable of working, yet refrains from taking part in income generating activities and leaves her to shoulder all responsibility.

Most women work in the unorganized sector. They invest little (as they have limited access to capital), and earn a pittance, their earnings are generally not consumerate with the labour and time spent in working. Yet, many daily commute to Imphal and the smaller townships or market centres, to sell their garden produce or manufactured good. Over the years, economic hardships have brought many Muslim women to directly participate in the market economy. Today, we see Muslim women vendors 'pot fambis', in most of the keithels in the valley of Manipur, selling vegetables and other food items. Lilong Keithel has around hundred to two hundred Muslim women of almost all age groups, selling commodities of daily consumption. Large numbers of Muslim women pot fambis are seen at Khwairamband. Many Muslim women also run pan-dukans, galamals, hotels, tailoring and embroidery establishments.[46]

Meitei women have been the solid bastion of Meitei culture and civilisaton. The Meitei kings were engaged almost in constant warfare with the neighbouring powers and the hillmen of the hills flanking the Imphal valley. Under the Lallup system, every Meitei male between the age of seventeen and sixty, was required to render free service to the king, for ten days in every forty. Besides, every male could be conscripted by the king for waging wars with other powers. This was possible, because the Meitei women, who were extremely industrious, used to perform the productive activities related to Agriculture, animal husbandry, cottage industry and internal trade, besides domestic chores. These constituted the mainstay of the Meitei Economy and therefore the role of women was of vital importance in keeping up the superstructure of Meitei state growth and expansion.[47]

History reveals that the institution of lallup enforced by Manipur's rulers from the eleventh century till the end of the eighteenth century, impacted women fundamentally in many ways. It compelled Manipuri women to single handedly assume responsibility on a dual front- the hearth, nurturing children and assuming domestic responsibilities, and out side the home Engaging in multifarious works which would bring in some revenue. Over and above, the Manipuri Burmese war of 1817 and the seven years devastation that followed it, decimated a good part of the male population, which was excacerbated by the Anglo-Manipuri war of 1891.[48]

In describing the position of women E.W. Dun writes: 'The women of Manipur, married or unmarried are not confined in zenanas, as they are in Bengal or Hindusthan; all classes are alike in this respect, neither do they cover their faces before strangers. They are very industrious, in this respect, the opposite of men, who are lazy and indolent. Most of the work of the country, except the heaviest, is performed by them, and they are consequently, the mainstay of the family circle. All the marketing is done by women, all the work of buying and selling in public, and the carrying to and fro of the articles to be sold; whilst at home they are busily employed in weaving and spinning. It would be difficult to find a more industrious woman in India than the Manipuri.[49]

Muslim women, sharing a common and unique bound with their non-Muslim sisters of the state, play an important role in the Economic sphere. It is a common sight in the rural areas to see Muslim women working in the paddy fields. Their labour is used in Agricultural operations like broad casting of rice seeds and its transplantation, harvesting, threshing, drying of paddy, and pounding. Except for ploughing they are engaged in the entire cycle of rice production and use. They also toil as hired labour for which they are paid on a daily basis, or in kind.

Rice is the main agricultural crop. Women worked in the paddy fields from early morning, preparing fields, sowing seeds, nurturing seed- beds, and transplanting seedlings, weeding etc. These activities were generally performed by women of a particular village in groups, the system being known as 'khutlang'. For harvesting crops, which called for mobilisation of a large work force, men joined women in completing the work quickly.[50]

Meitei women have been traditionally very good spinners of cotton yarn (like Muslim women in the Delhi sultanate). 'That woman (alone) is good who works all the time with the charkha (spinning wheel); for a seat of honour would deprive her of her reason'.[51] The family's requirement of cloth was met by women of the family who produced the materials on their own looms.

Cotton textiles woven by women included khesh, cloth of coarse quality, Muslin of fine quality worn as shawls by women, muslin of a little inferior quality used for turbans and jackets, and a variety of colourful dress materials. Johnstone, who served as Political Agent in Manipur applauded Manipuri women as highly skilled weavers who in many cases completely killed the manufacture of cloths peculiar to some of the hill tribes, over whom the Manipuri's had obtained mastery.[52]

Manipur produced a considerable quantity of silk textiles. Pemberton has praised Manipuri silk cloth for its strength and brilliance of colours. Petticoats, jackets and large scarfs were made of silk cloth for use as dress by both women and men. Embroidered silk cloth was in great demand in Burma. Silk cloth was also exported to Cachar in British India.

Leaves of mulberry plant were the sole feed of the silk worms. Mulberry, plants were raised in just five villages.[53] Edward Gait in 'A history of Assam' has cited that production of Manipuri silk was high as compared to China in the past. In 1763, the silk rate was Rs. 5/- per seer, but in 1873-74, 3 annas per seer.[54]

The Pangals had introduced a new loom – 'yong' as also new weaving designs. On the traditional loom they wove dolaiphi, kangthol phitha, for the exclusive use of the Muslims. They had learnt the technique of silk weaving from Bengal where the muslin production especially was of superior quality (Dacca muslins), Women earn on an average only about a thousand rupees a month from weaving, but even this meagre amount is an important addition to the family kitty.

T.C. Hodson wrote; 'Nearly every house wife is capable of weaving all the cloths needed by her family, and the simple loom stands in the verandah of the house. These cloths are mainly intended for wear, and not for decorative purposes'.[55] Different types of cloths may be grouped in to two categories (i) cloth for ordinary people which were simple and coarse, and cloth for the King, Royal family, dignitaries, prepared from silk and fine cotton with much embroidery. The process of cloth making involved spinning or making of yarn from the cotton, bleaching and dyeing, weaving, embroidery.

When cotton was grown or available the fibres were picked off with hand and twisted. Before the introduction of the ginning machine the cotton fibres were separated from the seeds, and twisting must have been done manually. After the yarn was prepared bleaching was done by application of cow dung, and in its absence green juice (chlorophyl) of plants was used. Frequent watering was done to release ozone. Other detergents used were soap nuts kekru, and the skin of the Heibi fruit. Colours for dyeing were obtained from the boiled extracts of barks of log wood called 'kuhi' and other trees, grass, flowers and clay. Working with the restricted tools and aids, an artisan could develop a highly mature colour pattern and aesthetic sense.[56]

The Muslim women are also adept at weaving, a skill handed down through generations. They produce cloth of variegated colours for own use and for sale, consisting primarily of chadars (khudei), phanek, shawls, bedding materials, mosquito nets, towels etc. Looms use to figure as an essential item of a Muslim bride. Divorced or widowed women often take up weaving to support themselves and their children.[57] However, today handloom products are losing ground; and preference is for manufactured textiles from outside the State, and durable, cheap cloth from Myanmar. But as traditional dress continues to be worn, there remains a steady market for such goods. However traditional bed sheets and cotton stuffed mattresses are being replaced by machine made bed sheets and mattresses, including attractive mattresses from Myanmar. The low cost of Myanmarese goods, and their colours and durability, are phasing out many traditional textile products.

The most striking feature of the Manipuri Muslim women's economic role is their direct participation in extra- familial economic activities. The performed the work of feeding and taking care of domestic animals- cows, buffaloes, ponies, goats, fowls, ducks, pigeons, Selling surplus agricultural, horticultural, and household industrial products, and buying goods for the family's consumption and meeting other needs were jobs exclusive to women. As the Meitei women worked more hours in farming than men, it was a 'Female Farming system' as defined by Esther Boserup.[57]

Muslim women are keen and energetic sales women, and possess a good sense of business. Not with standing, in many business transactions, they just manage to break even, not even making a minimum profit. The reason is probably their too low investment and money paid in transporting products from one place to another. Again, in an environment where there are frequent disruptions to law and order, Muslim vendors eager to reach home, before any untoward incident can occur, sell vast quantities of food commodities especially vegetables which easily spoil, at a very low price, especially as evening shadows lengthen. The customary practice is to group together a handful or more of a particular vegetable e.g. Tomato or ladyfinger, and offer it to customers at a flat rate of Rs. 10/-. This practice leaves no margin for profit but also enables the vendor not to fall into debt. This is important taking into account the high rate of interest on daily borrowings in the market place.

It is a common sight to have markets at convenient spots by the roadside (and more recently in not so convenient sites as the pedestrian pathway which becomes so constricted because of the presence of innumerable hawkers)- mainly or almost all women barring the Sunday market in which most sellers are males. Markets are also held in the village square where a group of Muslim women would assemble, either in the morning or evening, selling groceries, and all the basic commodities which they manage to amass from the adjoining villages. Miniature version of Khwairamband bazaar (women market) of Imphal can be seen in almost all the Muslim settlement areas. One of the biggest can be seen at Lilong, the highest Muslim populated area, six kilometers from Imphal. Here women vendors, occupying regular stalls sell almost every thing required for daily consumption, ranging from vegetables to rice, fresh and dried fish, Fruits, Eggs, oil, rugs, calico, sweetmeats, etc. Apart from its economic significance the market serves as an important institution of social and political interaction.[58] Women, because of the nature of their work, and because of their close proximity to each other in the market place, forge bonds, which give birth to a collective solidarity. For instance, in the Nupilal (women's war) of 1939, Muslim women joined Meitei women in Agitating against the British (protesting the export of rice). Similarly in the 18th June uprising 2002, Muslim women once again came to the forefront along with their Meitei sisters, although in this instance for a political reason. So also in the ongoing people's agitation of July 2009. The bonding that takes place among the women of the market place, is similar to the social and emotional bonding that occurs between men in their clubs.[59] The local markets also play an important role in rural development. Besides providing service and outlet for rural produce-these markets ensure the efficiency of the food distribution system, and inter-community linkages.[60]

Muslims had brought about technological innovations in the fields of spinning, cotton carding and weaving (the possible addition of treadles) in the medieval period, both in the Delhi Sultanate and the Mughal Empire. Women in Manipur have been known for their expertise in weaving. Muslim women use their limited free time to weave, as the earnings are a necessary, welcome addition to the family income. But they multitask, and cannot focus on weaving alone. On an average, they contribute through their family activities, an amount extending from ten to fifty percent of the total family income. Women in the higher paid remunerative jobs, including Grade IV employees in government service, contribute substantially to the family Exchequer. Teachers and Lecturers contribute even more. However the number of women in such services is abysmally low.

Because of financial constraints, even young Muslim girls-children in fact, work in the unorganized sector, selling vegetables or other commodities, assisting or managing Pan-dukans, and working in such crafts as embroidery, crocheting etc. young women are especially skilled in embroidery.

For purposes of marketing their wares, women commute by public transport (mainly buses, old jeep-taxis and Vans) to the towns; there after if they do not own or rent a stall in the market place they walk considerable distances from one leikei (neighbourhood) to another with a heavy basket of goods on their head, another one or two baskets in their hands, selling in each place they frequent. This hard work extracts a heavy toll on their physical well-being. They charge more than the market rate, but their profit remains meagre. In fact, women's contribution to the growth of Meitei economy as reflected in increased production of goods could be considered very high. Their participation in trade and exchange served as an important incentive to production of surplus. This was the significant propellant of growth and accumulation of wealth.[61]

Women become economically active generally at the age of fifteen. It is a common sight to see young, unmarried girls literally thrusting bunches of food stuffs, chiefly vegetables, at passersby. 25% of women above the age of fifteen are economically active. Poverty abounds in the rural areas, but no BPL survey has been conducted on gender basis, but approximately half of Muslim women must be BPL. Access to organised business up gradation of skills, training, is generally not available to women in the lower income bracket, largely because of lack of awareness of government schemes to empower them. Many young girls and women work on daily wages as domestic helps in urban households; there is no minimum ceiling on wages paid, they enjoy no leave or holidays, and what they receive is barely sufficient for their daily wants. But they are not in a position to bargain for higher wages, and are plagued with illiteracy. They enjoy no security, and are not protected by any insurance policy in case of accident, ill health, death etc. Many women work as daily wage labourers on construction sites. A few women in recent times, to garner additional income have even taken to selling illicit drugs, although drug use is either negligible or absent among Muslim women.[62]

Another deterrent to earning a sustainable livelihood is that the produce from kitchen gardens is sufficient only to meet the family's requirement and to sell in an adjoining village. Poor infrastructure, inadequate or in appropriate transport facilities (no refrigerated trucks or vans), and a late start in education are a cause of backwardness for Muslim women. Many of them earn a paltry sum of Rs. 1000/- in a month placing them below the poverty line. In the case of female workers, 41.40% are own account workers followed by 35.31% of them working in household enterprises as unpaid helpers. The percentage of women working as unpaid helpers is very high in Imphal West and Bishnupur districts, with 56.91% and 52.73% respectively, which is above the state average. 6.39% of the females are working as regular, salaried wage employees, as against 21.65% of their male counter parts.[63]

For too long, women in general have been considered appendages someone's daughter, wife, mother, sister, even when they earn an independent income or hold a position of authority at work. A field survey revealed that even highly educated Muslim women hesitate to answer any question related to research on Muslims in Manipur, and request the surveyor to approach their husbands. Women are natural 'nurturers', and 'care' responsibility is that of the women, but Pangal women like all other women Multi-task, and get a lot more work done in a day, than their male counterparts. But this is not taken into account while calculating the GDP. Women also manage time well. They also invest and save prudently if circumstances permit. Muslim women invest 30 to 40% of their earnings in traditional saving institution-Marups, which are like chit funds, but the interest on the money invested is little as the total sum invested is meagre. The larger the investment, the greater the returns. This institution helps in meeting both monetary and commodity needs at the time of life cycle rituals and socio-religious occasions, lean months, natural calamities like famine, crop failure, purchase of farm capital, implements, seeds, medical expenses, litigations.[64] Marup is the most popular form of saving among women in Manipur, from all strata of society. But today because of economic depression, inflation and absence of development, many thrift societies have become bankrupt as the members for various reasons are unable to contribute their due share regularly. (Daily, monthly, six-monthly, etc.) Still very often, saving for the marup enable crucial investment in the market place. Plots in the Ima Keithel are hereditary, and can

Montly Household Income Rs.	*Imphal East*	*Imphal West*	*Bishnupur*	*Thoubal*	*Churanchandpur*	*Chandel*	*Total*
Below 2000	35.04	49.24	36.77	45.19	27.77	28.90	41.23
2000-3000	28.42	24.07	27.48	18.23	28.41	45.09	23.35
3000-4000	12.90	7.89	14.46	7.67	17.05	13.01	10.09
4000-5000	4.31	5.39	6.20	7.01	21.59	5.76	5.88
5000-6000	6.24	3.70	3.72	8.43	5.68	4.34	6.80
6000-7000	3.95	4.01	2.48	4.68	0.00	0.00	4.13
7000-8000	2.75	2.00	2.27	2.89	0.00	1.45	2.67
8000-9000	1.70	0.62	1.45	1.66	0.00	0.00	1.53
9000-10000	1.38	0.77	1.45	1.26	0.00	1.45	1.26
10000-and above	3.35	2.31	3.72	2.98	0.00	0.00	3.06

also be purchased or rented. Muslim women hold plots or shares in the market place, although their number in proportion to the total number of women holding plots is about 20% but then Muslim women number only 1, 00,389. A few Pangal women take loans to finance their economic activities from credit societies and banks (more of the former), but the interest charged in usually exorbitant. The Meitei proverb: "Husband brings fire wood, wife brings all other goodies", is equally applicable to Muslim women.[65]

In the more recent past, some Muslim women and organisations have approached the government to fund schemes for development and economic empowerment. Many SHG's (Self help groups) have been formed, and are running successfully. But there is no social security scheme for women in the unorganized sector. However, there has been an attempt to induct women into computer training programmes, skills up gradation etc. Co-operative melas, which enable women to sell the goods they have manufactured, are also held at regular intervals. A Manipur Women Development Corporation also extends financial assistance to women entrepreneurs. In addition, 10% of the MOBC fund is spent on women's development- one example is the twenty lakh allocation for construction of a hostel for Muslim girls in 2001. But these measures remain inadequate as is illustrated by health-seeking behavior of Pangal women. Poverty adversely impacts on nutrition, makes health care largely unaffordable. (escalating cost of drugs medical procedures, admissions, operation), with the result, that many women suffer silently from preventable infections like T.B. diarrhoea, RTI's anemia, malnutrition etc., and are unable to function at their optimum level.

Another factor which largely impacts the purchasing power of Pangal women and affects adversely their livelihood is endemic, bandhs, general strikes, economic blockades, which occur at frequent intervals. Too many working days are lost in every calendar year. Deprived of their daily earnings, all too often, the women have no means to feed their family and themselves. Some studies have been made on loss of productivity, working hours, etc but not on a community basis.[66]

Taking into account the low representation of Pangal women in the employment sector (24.18%), with household sizes averaging 6.3 most households fall in the low income bracket. The number of affluent households is few; the highest annual income earning source is salaries, followed by wages, profits from entrepreneur enterprises and so on. The percentage of households by monthly household income in the districts of Manipur in 2004 is as follows.

From the above table it is apparent that as the income increases, the number of households decreases, with an exceptional indication in the income group of Rs.10, 000/-and above, in respect of Imphal East, Imphal West, Bishnupur, and Thoubal. In Churachandpur, no household has an income over Rs.6000 to 7000/-. Inequality of income can also be expressed as inequality in ownership of wealth, which is the net ownership of financial claims and tangible property. This table makes explicit the economic backwardness of the Meitei-Pangals as a whole, inclusive of women.[67]

References

1. Syed Ahmed – Status of Muslim Women in Manipur, p.51.

2. R. Brown – Statistical Account of Manipur, Delhi 1975, p. 85.

3. Gangmumei Kabui – History of Manipur, Vol.1, Pre-Colonial Period, p. 219.

4. Md.Latif Shah op.cit., p.198.

5. Thangjam Subhas Singh op.cit., pp.105, 107, cit. A.A. Howel- Short Account of Land Revenue in Manipur M.S. p. 9.

6. Gangmumei Kabui, op.cit. p. 220.

7. Thangjam Subhas Singh op.cit, p.114 cit. R.K. Sanahal Singh-Ed- Pangal Thorakpa, p. 21.

8. R.Brown, op.cit., p. 86.

9. Chandam Ragini Devi- The Economy of 18th Century Manipur- Unpublished M.Phil Dissertation 2008, Manipur University, p. 34, cit.N. Basanta- Socio-Economic Change in Manipur 1891-1947,1988, pp.13-14.

10. Report on Socio-Economic Survey of Meitei- Pangals, op.cit., p. 38.

11. E.W. Dun- Gazetteer of Manipur, Delhi 1981, pp. 60-61.

12. N. Wontharla- The Social and Cultural Life of Muslims in Manipur, Unpublished M.Phil Dissertation, Manipur University, 2008, p. 69 cit. Abdul Salam Md-Political Participation of Muslims in Manipur 1948, p. 33.

13. Jalad Baran Ganguly- An Economic History of North-East India 1826-1947, p. 287.

14. R. Brown, op.cit., p. 84.

15. J.B. Ganguly, op.cit, p. 289.

16. Chandam Ragini Devi, op.cit., p. 31.

17. J. B. Ganguly, op.cit., p. 289.

18. N. Wontharla, op.cit. pp.72-73 cit. Mhd. Waliallah Qazi, Written Manuscript, pp. 5-6.

19. A. Hakim Shah Khullakpam- The Manipur Governance to the Meitei Pangal 1606-1949, p.138.

20. Ibid., p.142.

21. N. Wontharla, op.cit., p. 86.

22. R. Brown, op.cit., p. 98.

23. N. Wontharla, op.cit., pp. 82-83.

24. A. Hakim Shah Khullakpam, op.cit., p.157.

25. Thangjam Subhas Singh, op.cit., p.125.

26. J.B. Ganguly, op.cit., p. 304.

27. Chandam Ragini Devi, op.cit. p.50, cit.J. Shakespeare- The Lushai-Kuki Clans, Cultural Publishing House, Delhi,1983, p. 30.

28. J.B. Ganguly, op.cit., p. 305.

29. Thangjam Subhas Singh, p.123 cit. R.K. Sanahal- Pangal Thorakpa 1985, p.16.

30. J.B. Ganguly, op.cit., p. 305.

31. Thangjam Subhas Singh p.122 cit. Thougal Masil, quoting Konsam Manikchand, p. 46.

32. Ibid, cit. Ningthourol Lambuba M.S.

33. J.B. Ganguly, op.cit., p. 306.

34. Thangjam Subhas Singh, p.124 cit. B.Khullachandra Sharma- Typology and Technology of Meitei Writing Materials, Imphal,1999, p.14.

35. N.Wontharla, op.cit. p.75, cit. Riyazuddin Chaudhury- Contribution of the Manipuri Muslims, pp. 2-3, 1988.

36. A. Hakim Shah Khullakpam, op.cit., p.165.

37. J.B. Ganguly, op.cit., pp. 306-307.

38. A. Hakim Shah Khullakpam, op.cit, p.141.

39. Ibid, p.155, cit. R.K. Sanahal Singh (ed) Pangal Thorakpa, No.10, p.15.

40. J.B. Ganguly op.cit., pp. 66-67.

41. Salam Irene- Manipur Muslim Women, p. 31.

42. Report on Socio-Economic Survey of Meitei Pangal 2004, op.cit., p. 42.

43. Salam Irene op.cit. p. 32 cit. Syed Ahmed- Status of Muslim Women in Manipur, p. 52.

44. Ibid.

45. Ibid., p. 53.

46. Syed Ahmed- Women Empowerment and Development op.cit., p.10.

47. J.B. Ganguly, op.cit., p. 8.

48. Syed Ahmed- Status of Muslim Women in Manipur, p. 54.

49. E.W. Dun- Gazetteer of Manipur, Delhi 1981, p.17.

50. J.B. Ganguly, op.cit., p. 68.

51. Cambridge Economic History Vol.1. Ed. by Dharma Kumar and Tapan Raychaudhury, p.78.

52. James Johnstone- Manipur and the Naga Hills, p. 97.

53. Ibid.

54. A. Hakim Shah Khullakpam, op.cit, p.143.

55. T.C. Hodson- The Meitheis, (1975), p. 27.

56. Haobam Shyamsunder- Art and Craft of Manipur. N. Sanajaoba (ed) Manipur Past and Present Vol. II, Delhi, 1991, p. 210.

57. Syed Ahmed, op.cit., pp. 54-55.

58. Ibid., p. 55.

59. Salam Irene op.cit., p. 33.

60. Syed Ahmed, op.cit.

61. J.B. Ganguly, p.70.

62. Salam Irene op.cit.p.34 cit. S.M. Islamuddin- Causes of Backwardness of the Manipur Muslim.

63. Report on Socio-Economic Survey of Meitei-Pangal 2004, op.cit., pp. 34, 36.

64. Syed Ahmed, op.cit., p. 56.

65. Salam Irene, op.cit., p. 35.

66. Ibid., p. 37.

67. Report on Socio-Economic Survey of Meitei Pangal, op.cit., p. 38.

4

Culture, Religion and Law

The culture of Muslims any where is based on: (i) the Islamic beliefs, way of life and code of ethics and (ii) on the influence of the indigenous civilization and custom of the people with whom they (the Muslims) live.[1] The second factor greatly influenced the culture of the Meitei-Pangals because in the first place, they made Manipur their home, secondly they married Meitei ladies and thirdly, they adopted the language and much of the traditions and customs of the Meiteis. The Muslims thus participated in the already existing life of Manipur and added to and enriched its culture, without changing its content, or impairing its structure. It formed a component part and became integrated, if not absorbed into the indigenous culture, which in its turn, formed an ingredient of the 'great culture' – A combination of diverse elements, contributed by the different units, each retaining its own shape and colour.

The Muslims of Manipur also inherited the cultural traits of their forefathers though not to the same extent as Muslims in other parts of India.[2] The Manipur Muslim women have more affinity with the Meitei women rather than Muslim women from outside Manipur. It may be said that the Muslim women's lifestyle is characterized by affinitive elements and the difference between Muslim women and the Meitei women, except in religious matters is only by degrees.[3]

The Muslims in Manipur like all communities in the state are fond of music, song, and to a lesser extent, dance. A community dance, similar to the Meitei 'thabal chongba', used to be performed on the night preceding a marriage. The most popular modes of music and song are the 'gajal', qawali (in Urdu/Persian), and ashemba eshei sung in Manipuri. The occasion of marriage presents a platform for the presentation of musical performances especially on the night preceding the wedding. While the dance is in progress, professional singers hired for the occasion sing Manipuri folk songs. Janab Khan opines that the dance style is that of 'Marbak'. But there is no concrete evidence to support this theory, as the dance performed by Muslims resembles the Meitei thabal chongba. According to Abdus Shahid Choudhury, merbak jagoi a dance without song is one of the favourite of Manipuri Muslim women. At the present time, religious leaders are trying to discourage these dances performed at the time of marriage, even though they are greatly enjoyed, especially by the young girls.[4] The Manipuri Muslim community has produced many singers of repute, especially in the realm of "Khullang Eshei".[5]

The major festivals of the pangals are the same as their co-religionists elsewhere. Cultural life largely centres around the celebration of three important religious festivals, which are observed with religious solemnity, and celebrated with gaiety and elan. The most important aspect of these festivals is the religious, which is observed with fervor. Only after the religious rituals are complete, celebrations follow. The festivals are Id-ul-filter, Id-ul-Zuha and Muharram. The first follows the month of Ramadan, alms are distributed, and prayers are offered by the Imam in congregation. Id-ul-Zuha is more elaborately celebrated as it is in commemoration of Abraham's Willingness to sacrifice his son Ishmael. Sacrifices of animals like cow or goat are made to God, thereafter; the flesh of the animal is distributed to relatives and people resident in the offeror's neighbourhood. In the festivals that follow the religious sacrifice many similarities to the Meitei celebration of Ningol Chakkouba can be observed. (Feast for married sisters and daughters) This primarily consists in the offering of food and gifts, Just as in Ningol Chakhouba, married daughters and sisters visit their natal homes, with offerings of coconut, fruit and sweetmeats, and are in turn feted, given a lavish repast and gifts so also married women accompanied by their children, visit their parents home, attired in bright, new clothes. Much attention is paid to the cuisine on these festive occasions, and family members and guests, partake of many delicacies, dressed in new clothes, bought specifically for the occasion.

Prior to the start of Ramadan, Talpiba is observed. Women of each locality together prepare 'tal' cakes, made of rice, and other sweets, which are distributed among neighbours, as also the poor. 'Thoutal' and 'Maroital', are some of the varieties of cakes, prepared by the Manipuri Muslim women.[6]

Muharram is as its name implies, a solemn festival, during which groups of elderly people gather at the Mosque and pray in the form of mourning for the sacrifices, made by the followers of Ali.

'Jalsah' occupies a vital place in the Realm of cultural life. The annual Jalsah is a must for every Manipuri Muslim inhabited areas, where religious scholars, orators, social activists, deliver lectures on topics of religion, and discuss problems pertaining to society and culture. Jalsah is eagerly awaited, and is usually held in the time of leisure i.e. the post-harvest period. The recitation of gajal, qawali, nat-e-rashul, hamd in Manipuri, along with a shemba eishei, form an intrinsic part of the jalsah celebration. Most singers on such occasions are reputed professionals. Muslims from far and wide are invited to a charity feast, symbolizing community solidarity and consciousness. Over the years, Jalsah has become an important socio-religious gathering of the Muslims.[8]

With reference to architecture, although initially the Muslims followed the principles of house construction of the Meiteis, in recent times, most of the newly constructed buildings, private and public, especially masjids and madrasas, bear symbols and motifs and techniques of traditional Islamic architecture, as for instance, the principle of the arch and dome that the Turks brought into North. India in the thirteenth century, minarets, symbols of the crescent moon and star, floral designs, arabesque decorations and calligraphy (inscribing Quranic Verses). Since most of the dwellings of the Muslims are not pucca, these techniques and styles can be used only in limitation.

However, the madrasas at Lilong, and the imposing masjid at Babupara, in the heart of Imphal city, bear witness to the use of traditional Islamic architectural designs and techniques.[9]

In the field of language, the Muslims have enriched the vocabulary of the state. They introduced a new etiquette and forms of salutation, borrowed from Arabic, Urdu, Farsi. Phrases and words like 'Aslamu-Alaikum' (May God bless you), walekum salam (May you be blessed), Khuda hafiz (goodbye), insallah (god-willing), imam (faith), khuda (creator), hajrat (Respected), musafah (greetings/handshake), subhanallah (Exclamation), quam (Community), began to be increasingly used in place of traditional Meitei greeting terms. Many Urdu words soon became assimilated into the Meitei vocabulary. Some such words, spoken by both communities in common often daily usage are : chalak (cunning), masala (spice), dukan (shop), hafta (week), rumal (handkerchief), parda (curtain), dag (stain), moza (socks) khabar (news), tarikh (date), kamiz (shirt) etc. The Manipuri Muslims use in addition certain urdu words or words derived from urdu, such as 'Hella' from Hai Allah, Bei- a word derived from Bahin (sister), chora – a word derived from Chidiyan (small bird) and Gaya – a word derived from Goiyan (a woman's female friend). They also have coined words such as Ichamba (Icha Manba), Ithou (Ibok) etc. But enrichment of language is most evident in the folk songs composed by Muslims in Meitei lon. In earlier times, Muslim ladies sang such songs, accompanied by dance at the time of wedding, the rendition of such songs evoked emotional reactions, smiles and tears. The bride too, joined in the singing, as she bade farewell to her parents, relatives and friends.

The songs express the love of parents for children and vice-versa, as also the feelings associated with pangs of separation.[10]

Some words however, were a combination of Urdu and Meitei words. As for example : Dadash + Ahal = Dahal-elder brother, Bahin + ahal = Bei hal – elder sister and Hanum + Hanba – derivation from Hinam and hanba – return of bride and groom to bride's parent's residence, after three, or five or seven days of marriage. Other words were independently coined, such as Ichamba, mentioned above – an address to a son of a distant brother in the same sagei, ithou-ibok-grandmother. The Muslims in addition used words slightly different from the Manipur equivalent, lapkang for leikang (soot), ipunga for ipuwa (younger brother), mayem for mayum (house), and kanthra for kantha (quilt).[11]

But even before the Muslims came to Manipur in 1606 A.D., Urdu was used in the kingdom. Manipur maintained relations with the king of Bengal. In 1514 A.D. a letter was sent in Persian (Urdu) script by the king of Bengal Hussein Shah (1493-1518) to the Manipur king Lam Kyamba (1512-1523). According to 'Lairik Yengbam Lon' the king of Manipur sent three Manipuris to Tripura, to fetch a scribe to read it. They brought Kavi Chandra in 1514 A.D.

As a matter of fact, Meitei Pangals received education in two languages: Arabic was necessary for Islamic study, being the language of the Quran and Hadith; Meiteilon was used as a medium of communication – moreover, it was the official language. In the seventeenth century, the Meitei Pangals probably learnt Meiteilon, with writing in Bengali characters through the Agency of persons such as Muhammad Sani, Syed Ambiya, Syed Abdullah, Syed Hussein, Sheikh Zunneid/Chuleiya, Sifar Muhammad Sheikh Sei Janat, Syed Siliman, (Suleiman), Syed Ngangba, Sheikh Noori, etc. Besides, there was a Lairikyengbam clan of the Meitei-pangal. Their forefathers were Walli Khan Malik khan and Bahadur Khan.[12]

Outdoor Sports and Indoor Amusements

As early as the reign of Khagemba there were two Muslim wrestlers, Akun Shah and Kanba Shah attached to the king's palace. The tradition of wrestling was continued by their successors who came to be known as the Mansham Sagei (Wrestling clan). The existence of institutions like the Pangal Loisang, Shinglup, Keirup and Leirup, encouraged and facilitated sport among the Pangals. Two games known as 'Likkon Shan Naba and Kang Shannaba' were played with the Meiteis; however Pangal women did not play kang. Many Pangals kept a kang in their homes for playing. They also played shagol-kangjei, mukna, mukna-kangjei, khong kangjei, yubi-lakpi and were split into two groups known as 'Khun thak and Khunkha' and 'Ahall-up and Naharup. It would seem that these divisions were based on locality because when there was a competition organized between the panas, the Pangals were included in the pana of the Meiteis, which was adjacent to their settlement; special dresses were worn for different sports.

In the sport of polo-shagol kangjei, some Muslims were prominent, for e.g. A Pangal noble Walliullah who was a darbar member, and played the sport together with Britishers and the Meiteis at Mapal Kangjeibung (polo field at Imphal). Some villages produced sportsmen like Yairipok, Irong, Heiyel Labuk, Kwakta etc. One Sanggai-Yumpham played at Awang Sabal, and participated in competitions. Other noted players were Abdul Jabar (Hui Faba), Usmaan, Md. Hamukpa, Ahsanullah, Suhaib Ali, Jaan Ali (Jaali), Jaman and the popular Md. Ebadullah.

The first to play football among the Muslims was Md. Hussain of Lilong Bazar, who played for the town club. To excel in the sport, he followed the practice of jogging from Lilong upto the football ground at Kalimai Lampak. This enabled him to retain a good form for the sport. Other well-known footballers were Nazir Ali of Keikhu, Rousan Ali of Kairang, Najibun Hussein of Khergao, Karimuddin Alias Angoubi of Porompat.

In the game of hockey, Najir Ali of Keikhu was the pioneer player who commenced playing in the 1930's. He had the distinction of playing for the Beighton Cup in Calcutta and the Manipur Olympic Games in 1949, representing the town club. A Muhammadan sporting Union Board was established in 1939 at Khergao, it soon became very popular. Its notable players were Najir Ali, Naqi Ahmed (Freedom fighter), Hussamuddin, Anwar Abdul Haque of Keikhu, Halim Choudhury (IAS retired) of Babupara, Najibun Hussein, Rashid, Nejam Zia, Mansur Ali, Manab, Hasan, Maneruddin (Advocate), Riazuddin Choudhury of Khergao, Roushan Ali of Kairang, Abdul Ali of Pangong, Rahman Kshetri Idgah Road, Ali of Kshetri-mayai. The sporting union emerged as the champion in the local league in 1948. Unfortunately, it ceased to exist after 1949. Of these players, Halim Choudhury played in 1946 for the

Churachand team and the town club, and in 1948 for eastern sporting union; he also participated in the Beighton Cup in Calcutta in 1949.

In the field of Athletics, 2 Muslim brothers-Md. Ali and Md. Tomba, won the first and second places in the sports meet held at the palace ground – Hafta Kangjeibung, organized by the Maharaja Churachand Singh, Md. Rafe of Lilong Turel Ahanbi won the marathon (Forty miles) in 1948.

In Mukna Kangjei and Lamhai Kanjei, Amerullah and Saferuddin of Kshetri Iri Mapal excelled. These sports were participated in prior to Manipur's merger into the Indian Union in 1949.

With the changes brought about by the merger, recreational sports associated with marriage ceremonies, and the Eid festival, registered a sharp declinc. But games like football, hockey and volley ball became increasingly popular, and sports organizations came into existence at the village level. Muslims joined other sports organizations as well. They competed too in sporting events organized by educational institutions.

Some names stand out in this post-merger period for various sports. Halim Choudhury, a prominent member of the Manipuri Muslim community was a member of the Manipur hockey team that played in the Beighton Cup in Calcutta in 1951, whereas Md. Jabbar represented the Imphal College in 1957 and in 1959, particularly in the Inter College sports festival at Guwahati. In the second inter-college district hockey tournament at Silchar in 1959, in which Manipur emerged victorious, Halim Choudhury captained the team, and another player was Najibun Hussain of Khetrigao. Md. Jabbar was a member of the hockey team that played in Delhi in 1965.

Roushan Ali, Najibun Hussain, Jabar, Abdul Qadir of Kshetri Mayai, Najir Ali, Sahidur of Kshetri Iril were prominent in football in the 1950's. And in 1955, the friends Athletic sports organization of Kshetri Iril Mapal came second in the Maharaja Budhachandra Memorial Football Cup. An association, Athletic Brothers Association was founded in 1968 and emerged champion in 1973 and 1983. Some Muslims were members of the Eastern Sporting Union, Young Physique Union, Manipur Rifles, etc.

A good footballer was Md. Itomba who played for Eastern Sporting Union in 1972 and represented Manipur at Agra in 1974, in Bihar in 1975, in the All India School competition as Vice-captain in 1977, the Sanjay Gandhi Memorial competition in 1972, in Orissa as captain of Manipur's junior team in 1979, in the Santosh Trophy in 1981. Md. Tayeb Ali of Hafiz Hatta was a prominent National player.

The Muslim women did not lag behind. Fatima Begum of Kshetri Awang leikai was a member of the India eleven team that played at Bhirt Nagar, Nepal in 1975. She participated in the Kamala Nehru Trophy at Allahabad in 1978. She captained the Manipur team that played against the UK football team at Imphal. She participated in national women's championships held at Kerala, Ahmedabad, Jammu, Amrabati etc. She completed a one year physical education course from Pune in 1989. Fatima was the first Muslim player of the North-East in this discipline.

Khut-heibam Nazima Begum of Kshetri Mayai participated in the sub-junior national women's football camp at Sasaram in 1987 and the tenth Junior National Women's football camp, Deoria in 1989, more women began to take part in sports in the 1970's and 1980's. There is no prohibition to women's participation and Pangal women were influenced by the Meitei, and encouraged to take an active part in sports.

Halim Choudhory as also other Muslims – Ramjan of Kshetri Awang, Anwar and Rashimuddin of Kshetri Mayai Leikai were appointed as refrees. The first played an active role in sporting unions that sprang up.

Of polo players in 1953 and 1954, Alimuddin of Sangai yumpham occupies an important place. Md. Ningthem of Heiyel Loubuk,, Ali and Qarab of Irong, Abdul Jalil of Kwakta, Asad, Usmaan, Umeed Ali, Manu, Turaf Salam Turaf, Tomcha Haji, Nur, Ali, Nur Muhammad, Imammullah, Md. Ali, Tame, Mane of Sangai Yumpham, Ethouba and Abdul Wahid of Kshetri Iril are contemporary polo players. An international player was Abdullah of Paobitak (1990). Md. Ladu of Yairipok excelled in the game, Polo organisation were formed at Yaripok, Paobitak, Sangai Yumpham, Irong, Thoubal, Kwakta etc. Most participated in polo tournaments held at Imphal.

Other great sportsmen were Md. Tombi of Khergao Sabal leikai, who won a walking race, Fatima Begum in racing and Md. Tayeb Ali (Marathon of 26 miles). In other games too, like shot-put, disc throw and javelin, Fatima Begum excelled. This only proves that Muslim women possess the potential to reach the top in sports.

In Mukna or Meitei style wrestling, Md. Latif (ex-MLA) won the Manipur Mukna Jatra, it was won in 1958-59 by Md. Manab of Khergao, Volleyball became entrenched in the villages of Lilong, Yairipok, Sangai Yumpham, Khetrigao and Kairang, whereas in arm-wrestling the champion was Md. Arasddin of Khergao, winning in Calcutta the world championship (45 kg. category) 1986, in London in 1987 and Mexico 1985.

In martial arts, a popular sport, Md. Tala Ahmed of Wangoi won the National championship in Bombay in 1984, and in Karate, Md, Abdul Kalam of Keirang Litan Makhong in black belt at Imphal in 1992. In weight lifting, Abdul Hashim of Keikhu won in Madhya Pradesh in 1991, participated in Ahmedabad 1992, Calcutta in 1993, Asansol in 1993, and secured first position in state level competition at Imphal.

The above name of sports persons of the Meitei-pangal community, illustrate the latent talent of the Muslim community. But because of various factors like economic backwardness, corruption in fund management etc. participations of Muslims is on the decline, even though infrastructure and training in sports disciplines is on the rise.[12]

Religion : Like the Turks of Central Asia, who established an empire in India in the thirteenth century and the Mughals who followed them in the sixteenth century, and who made India their home, the Muslim who came to Manipur from 1606 onwards, made Manipur their home. In the process of their settlement, they adopted and assimilated much of Manipur's culture; they married local Meitei women, adopted meiteilon as their mother-tongue and lived side by side in harmony with the Meiteis. The degree of assimilation and inculturation was extremely high. But what distinguished these Muslims was their profession of the Islamic faith. However the early settlers were not prosleytisers and did not make an attempt to propagate Islam. Among the Muslims, religion regulates both sacred and secular practices. Religion will shift from being a peripheral to a central issue, when local elites attempt to out bid each other in an effort to increase their religious legitimacy, with an internal and in many but not all cases an external audience.[13] Dun asserted however, that 'the Muhammadans of this country (Manipur), are very ignorant of their religion.[14] So also Mc Culloch writes : 'Whole Mussalman population being very ignorant of the creed they profess, is not attended with the inconvience which it would be amongst a better informed people.[15] The Muslims were liberal and unorthodox, had no Masjid. This stage maybe called 'Semi-Islamic' or 'Sub-Islamic period, as it was largely influenced by the local culture and customs of Manipur valley. This period lasted from the middle of the seventeenth century to the end of the nineteenth century. At that time, there was no evidence of the existence of a priestly class among the Pangals.[16] Kheiruddin Khullakpam disagrees. 'The Muslims had a Masjid since their arrival in Manipur. Abdullah Shaheed was the first Maulvi after the seven years devastation of Manipur.[17] The Nongsamei states that Syed Hussen brought the Quran to Manipur in 1608. Maulvis made their appearance a little before Manipur came under colonial rule.[18] The Muslims adopted Islam in a strict manner after 1910 A.D. prior to 1910 A.D. there were no hard and fast rules with regard to religion and faith. Even the purdah system was not practiced then, but in later years after 1910, some enlightened Muslims began to educate their people about the teachings of Islam. Following the dictums of religion, the female members began to be confined in the four walls of their households. But as time passed, their relatively worsening economic condition compelled the female members and even the children, to cross the thresholds of their houses to make ends meet.[20]

Although the Manipur Muslim may not in general be inspired by missionary zeal, Muslims strictly adhere to the tenets of Islam, and disregard of compulsory religious obligations invites social ostracism. It is true that 'the mosque had always been the principal public institution in Islamic civilization. It is the physical embodiment of the social reality of Islam, and hence the paramount institution, by which community identity and solidarity are expressed. This is especially true of the 'Friday' or congregational mosque, in which Muslims gather once a week for a sermon read by one of its functionaries.[21] It is the foremost Islamic institution, and although women are excluded from the religious services, at home, they instruct their off-spring in moral and spiritual values and practices, and often engage learned scholars to teach Islam in the home. There may be no women's mosques, but a room is set apart for women in the Jama Masjid in Imphal. It is strictly screened from the section where men offer namaz.

Islam was the last of the great, modern world religions. Religious values are deep rooted and the Meitei-Pangal believes in the same Islamic doctrine as their co-religionists elsewhere believe in. The word

'Islam' itself means to submit to the will of God. Muslims in Manipur honour Muhammad, 'the apostle of God'. They believe that the Quran is the revealed word of God; the first message of God was brought by the Angel Gabriel to Muhammad : La-Ilaha-Illallah, Mudhammadur-rasul-Allah- There is no God but Allah, Mohammad is the messenger of Allah. Muhammad is revered as the last great Prophet of the one and only God. Belief in Allah means faith in God and his attributes of: life (Hayat), Knowledge (Ilm) Power (Qudrat), Will (Irada), Hearing (Sama), Sight (Basar) and Speech (Kalam). The Manipuri Muslims also adhere to the five basic principles of Islam: Yashahhud (witnessing through the creed), Salat (prayer five times a day), Saum (fasting during the entire month of Ramadan), Zakaat (Almsgiving), and Hajj (pilgrimage to Mecca). The obligatory congregational prayer on every Friday noon and the Id prayers are offered in the mosque. Id prayers can also be offered at the Idgah. The five hours prescribed for obligatory prayers are Fazr (dawn), Zohr (noon), Asr (late afternoon), Maghrib (sunset) and Isha (night). The place where Muslims gather for worship is known as the 'Masjid' Its head is an Imam-who imparts instructions to boys and girls on the Quran; in the mamang shangoy (a covered open construction in front of the house) or in the verandah which serves as a maktab. Mode of payment was paddy, rice or money, agreed to by both parent and teacher. In the seventeenth century with the entry of educated Syeds a spurt was given to Islamic education of Meitei Pangals. The call for prayer is given in a loud voice in Arabic. When 'Muslims pray, no music is played nor a song or hymn sung-neither are offerings or collections taken, Friday is a sacred day when Muslims assemble in the mosque. For Congregational noon prayer is obligatory for all adult males. The Id prayers are offered in the morning, sometime after the Morning Prayer, but before the noon prayer. Whenever a Muslim meets another Muslim, he greets him with the words 'Assalamu Alaikum'-peace be upon you, and the person greeted replies 'wa alaikum assalam'-peace be upon you also. Fasting during Ramadan is binding on all adults. Almsgiving purifies the giver, and blesses his possessions. It can be given in cash or kind. It is obligatory on Muslims who can afford it, to make the pilgrimage to Mecca. The pilgrim on return is addressed as 'Haji'.

The reading of the Quran is obligatory, Muslims in Manipur for a long period, emphasized the importance of religious studies. They perceived education as inculcation of knowledge that concerns the faith only.[22] Moreover, due to lack of proper information about the Quran and Hadith, and lack of uniformity in the exposition of their meaning, women have been denied their rights. Overs and above, social customs, poverty, illiteracy, also often erode or subvert Quranic intents.[23]

A network of madrassas came into existence. The madrassa, although largely disseminating religious education is not perceived as a threat in any way. It is viewed as an educational institution of a religious minority, who observe Friday as a holiday. In recent times, madrassas have tried to adopt the syllabus of government schools, inclusive of computer education.[24] The Ulema however emphasise that religion should be the basis of ordering the socio-economic and collective life of the Muslims. They fail to comprehend the dimensions of real socio-economic and political problems. The Ulema, mostly graduated from the madrassas of Delhi, Meerut, Rampur, Shaharanpur, Cachar etc. through the medium of their apex body, Jamiat-ul-Ulema, started to rejuvenate the true Islamic tradition in Manipur. The Jamiat works for the propagation of Islam. And its values, to secure and safeguard the religious, educational, cultural and civil rights of the Muslims, revival of Islamic and Arabic studies, educational and socio-religious reform of Muslims, to promote communal harmony in the state. They also introduced Islamic and Muslim dress code, manners, etiquette etc.[25] But because of assimilation in Manipuri society, most Muslims favor Meitei dress, and a Manipuri Muslim women leader was of the view that the 'Phanek' (sarong) and 'Khudei' (lungi) were within the purview of the purdah, as they both covered the body.[26] The purdah system is not strictly enforced among Manipur's Muslims. But they are not permitted to expose their bodies to strangers, and even distant relatives. They have recourse to a veil when moving in the public sphere. In every Muslim village or leikai, there is a Masjid. The first Masjid was erected in 1896 at Babupara. The Masjid at Minuthong Golapati, and that at Lilong, are large in size.

Islam is not a prosleytising religion, nevertheless there have been conversions from among the meiteis and tribals, though not to any appreciable degree. The non-Muslim spouse embraces Islam on marriage, and children are brought up as Muslims.

One of the most significant contributions of the Jamait is the establishment of a chain of madrassas. The Jamiat serves as the Board for the madrassas in

Manipur. The first madrassa, Lilong LP madrassa was established in 1907. In 1980, Darol-Uloom, one of the biggest madrassas in Manipur was established at Lilong Haoreibi, on the line of Darul-Uloom of Deoband. The madrassa has four branches and around eight hundred boarding and non-boarding talbas (students). The madrassa also runs a yatimkhana (orphan home). The madrassa has constituted a body of Ulemas-Dar-Al-Ifta; to issue registered fatwas[27] (A decision based on the shariat is known as fatwa). But as a distinguished Manipuri Muslim academician phrased it: 'Religious functionaries only adjudicate religious disputes, secular issues are decided by civil courts, power of the former decreasing in inverse proportion to increase of power of the latter.[28]

Every year, the madrassas organize jalsa. But the main concern of the madrassas is to produce maulvis. These institutions, despite short comings, remain the only source of education for poor families and orphans. Islam is deeply entrenched, and does not need to be revived. Yet a divide occurred between the Meitei and Pangal communities, when the Meiteis converted to Hinduism in the eighteenth century, and the Pangals began to be looked down upon.[29] This development, perhaps acted as an incentive on the Muslims, to become more fervent in prayer and to engage themselves in a quest for identity. They began a study of religious works, and many Muslims decided to become Maulvis. The first Maulvi of Manipur, viz. Tanjou Moulvi came from Cachar, and settled at Thoubal Moijing. He was a Cachar Pangal and belonged to the Moijing clan. The second and third Maulvis also were from the same place. Subsequently prominent Maulvis viz Maulana

Meinoruddin and his brother Moulana Rahimuddin were born there. Both Maulvis and Moulanas were accorded great respect and honor, and occupied a privileged position in society. But this position has been gradually eroded as the result of the emergence of a new class of Muslims, comprised of government officers and employees, academicians, entrepreneurs and businessmen.[30]

Syed Shahabuddin (Muslim India, 108, Dec.1991:531) declared "For a Muslim at the personal level, his religious identity is supreme, rising above race, language, geography or political jurisdiction. Indeed, he is not prepared to trade his religious identity for any price" Two schools of thought emerged from among the Muslims in Manipur with their own set of modus operandi. The religiously trained Muslims or Ulema represent one group. They believed that the only way to regain their status and glory was by looking inward, identifying the wrongs, and dealing with them within the framework of the Quran and Hadith. Islamic institutions became a bastion of traditionalism; the main concern of the madrassas was to produce Muslim scholars (Maulvis), who would perform various ecclesiastical functions, such as Imams, Hafizs, Qaris, Khatibs and Ustads. The curriculum followed in these institutions called Dars-i-Nizami included Quranic recitation, Quranic exegesis, hadith, jurisprudence, logic, history, Arabic grammar, lexicography, Rhetoric, prosody and literature.[31]

Tabaligh movement is popularized in Manipur in recent times by the Ulema, and talbas associated with Dar-Uloom madrassa; the madrassa is also the markaz (head quarters) of Tablighi Jamaat. The movement is aimed at creating a sense of community solidarity and religiosity, by exhorting its followers to imbibe the letter and spirit of the Quran and Hadith, and to follow the standards of an ideal life set by the Prophet and his companions, and work for the realization of an Islamic ideal. The Jamaatis roam from village to village (Safr), preaching these ideals. They hold ijtima or religious conclave annually, to discuss matters relating to faith, Jamaat, and society. Thousands of Muslims from far and wide gather together in these congregations, including renowned Jammatis (Bujurk), from other parts of India. The Jamaatis have also become sensitive to setting right, ills that plague the Pangal society, especially drug-use, through a process of counselling and rehabilitation. Not only these reformed youth but educated unemployed and frustrated youth are also involved in Jamaati activities.[32]

Although the Pangals are strict followers of Islam, Muslims in general are not orthodox, especially the young, and many do not abide strictly by the regulations. The elders and Maulvis however influence some Muslims to repent for their sins (taubah).[33]

A Manipur Wakf Board was constituted in 1988 to manage the wakf (endowment) to Masjids, madrassas, idgahs, kabarstans and other properties used for religious and pious purposes and recognized by Muslim law. The Board also provides financial assistance to needy Muslims. Similarly, a Manipur Haj Committee was constituted in 2003, to enable Muslims to make the pilgrimage to Mecca. The scene of pilgrim departure from Imphal airport en route to Mecca is charged with religious and emotional sentiments. Every pilgrim is garlanded and recites 'Labbaik'-Here, I come; family members, relatives and friends exchange musaffa (handshake) with the pilgrim. Special arrangements are made to facilitate the attainment of haj.[34]

In public religious rituals, Pangal women do not play an important role, in contrast to the leading role performed by Meitei maibis (priestesses) at the Lai Haoraba festival of the Meiteis. Even though Islam believes in equality, women in practice, do not enjoy equal status with their husbands, and so do not participate with men on an equal footing in the performance of religious rituals. For non-Muslim women who convert to Islam on marriage, there is a problem of lack of knowledge of Islam its laws, practices, customs and traditions. They often find themselves at a loss when faced with adjustments to a different culture, religion and way of life, and have great difficulty in adapting to the different ways of worship, of living, of socio-religious norms. Generally Muslims today obliterate such difficulties and for religious and other reasons, marry within their own community, unlike in the seventeenth century when Muslim men married Meitei women. Although not playing a pivotal role in religious rituals, Muslim women perform the duties of ritual cleansing of the home, preparing and laying out garments ready for use, preparing the special food delicacies associated with festivals like Id. There is however, a great chasm between theology, scriptures and practice, as the illiterate Muslim rural women are still largely ignorant of the finer points of religion and law.[35]

But all Muslim children of seven to eight years are taught Arabic in the local maktabs by a Maulvi in a co-educational set-up. Writing in Arabic is compulsory. All Muslim women learn Arabic, although all do not get a general education. On attaining adolescence girls are taught hymns for prayer at home by their mothers or female relatives. If the adolescent girls do not get proper knowledge of prayer from their mother, a local Maulvi is arranged to teach them well, on condition of public payment. All women from the age of thirteen onwards, perform prayer five times daily inside the house, after cleansing their bodies, and attiring themselves in clean clothes. During the month of Ramadan, they continue their daily prayer schedule, despite having to labour to prepare meals at sunset and before sunrise. Muslim women who have made the Haj are known as 'Hajibi'. They become spiritually stronger after the pilgrimage. They are accompanied by their husband, father, son or brother, as they cannot travel unaccompanied by a male relative. When death occurs in a family, it is the women who wash and clean the corpse before it is brought to the mosque.[36]

Law: The source of Muslim Law is the Quran, Hadith, Ijma and Kyas. It is not customary to talk of modern sources of Muslim Law, since the Muslim jurists admit of no modification by any earthly agency. But the fact of the matter is that Muslim law has undergone modifications throughout the period of British rule. The vehicles of these modifications have been three: (a) doctrine of equity, justice and good conscience (b) precedent and (c) legislation. Muslim personal law is not misused but it not applied. For instance, consent of the first wife must be taken before a man marries a second time. And it is incumbent to maintain equality in maintenance allowance to all wives. The share of inheritance to which a daughter is entitled is often not given in practice. Also Muslims indulge in practices prohibited by Islam e.g. drinking gambling drug-trafficking, taking interest on money lent etc.[37]

The personal law of the Muslims is applied to marriage, dower (mehr or mahr), dissolution of marriage, percentage and legitimacy, guardianship and maintenance gifts, wakfs, pre-emption, and wills and gifts. It also includes intestate succession, special property of females, personal property inherited or obtained under contract or gift.

The Muslim Personal Law Shariat Act of 1937 (MPLA), and the Dissolution of Muslim Marriage Act of 1939 (DMMA), which have been the crucial legislations of the Muslim family law, were both introduced during the British period. In addition, we now have the Muslim Women (Protection of Rights on Divorce) Act 1986. A personal law be that part of the community laws that govern personal, affairs like marriage dower, legitimacy, custody, succession to property. It is different from non-personal laws which govern all within the national boundaries like Criminal Law. It governs a person because he/she belongs to a particular religion, race, caste, sect or tribe.[38]

As per the laws of Islamic jurisprudence, the Pangals are not to have recourse to usury, yet they do practice this and also charge exorbitant rates of interest. But the larger majority emulates the Meiteis and rather than dealing with banks, they save, invest money in traditional thrift societies or marups. At the present time, many Pangals have opened bank accounts, the money deposited accrues interest, but Muslims do not hesitate to avail of this advantage. Traditionally, there are two categories existing, the first 'Bai' or financial transaction is permitted by the Quran whereas the second form known as 'Riba', interest on money lent, is illegal. There is no conclusive evidence that interest given by a bank comes under the category of 'Riba', it may be more akin to 'shirka' or 'mudaraba' (which is lawful in Islam) there is a similar uncertainity surrounding the validity of insurance.[39]

Similarly, in the sphere of family planning Muslims have to observe the Islamic injunction that the purpose of marriage is procreation, so birth control would not be ordinarily permitted. However, in the changed circumstances of today, it is permitted for valid reasons, be it physical or economic reasons. The use of this measure is a private matter between husband and wife, and the method of birth control resorted to, must be least injurious or harmful.[40]

Inheritance is governed by the Shariat Act of 1937. Muslims of Manipur inherit movable and immovable properties from their parents. A portion of the property is to be kept reserved for daughters and wives. Under Islamic law, the mother, wife and daughter are legal female heirs. The maximum share of the mother is one-third, and minimum one-sixth, depending on the number of heirs. The share of the wife is one-fourth or one-eighth, depending on the number of children and grandchildren. The wife is also the owner of mehr, and entitled to be maintained by her husband. A daughter is a primary heir like the son. Her share fluctuates, depending upon the number of surviving children, grand-daughter from a daughter; however it does not stand on a par with the grand-daughter from a son.[41]

The Muslim law prohibits the use of certain foods as also intoxicants, and there is a clear distinction between 'halal' and 'haram'. For instance, Muslims are not allowed to eat pork, and the Pangals adhere to this regulation.

Women and the Shariat – Women are at a disadvantage and inferior in legal status, with special reference to marriage, divorce, adoption and guardianship of children, maintenance and inheritance. In analyzing the position of women in Muslim society, one has to take into account the rights granted by Islamic doctrine, and the actualities of the present condition. The Islamic doctrine embodying the teachings of the Quran and traditions of the prophet (Hadith), constitute an important source of the status and position of women. The Islamic doctrine therefore provides the legal normative postulates. However, a distinction should be made between the Islamic doctrine and Islamic i.e. those customs which are inherited by and not invented by the Muslim society. A number of customs now treated as Quranic, have nothing to do with Islam. These customs and practices have been the features of the social life of people who did not abandon them after embracing Islam, and have adopted certain cultural forms of the dominant Hindu community.[42] The first Muslim women in Manipur in the seventeenth century were converted Meitei women who brought with them, their own customs and rituals.

There were a number of religious taboos. When Iroiba Yumjao of Kontha Ahallup married a Meitei-Pangal woman, he was boycotted by his community and settled among the Meitei Pangal in 1870. So also Yellangbam Maibi in 1871. Another instance is that of a Meitei Pangal and a Meitei from Takhellambam drinking water from the same glass in public. The latter was ostracized, and began living with the Meitei Pangal from 1873. Similarly Loitomcha Tanjao had to settle with the Meitei Pangal in 1875. Shagolsem Thambal, a beautiful maiden married Usman, a handsome tailor in 1880. Her parents were compelled to settle in Lilong Wangma Pangal Khullak. This love story is still narrated by the Meitei Pangals. In 1885, a man of the Seram clan of Urup married a Meitei Pangal woman and had to settle with the Meitei Pangals in Urup, so also in 1903, a man of Akangjam of Khurai who married a Meitei-Pangal settled among them. Wahengbam Madhop of Kontha Ahallup married a Meitei Pangal and settled at Kairang in 1926.[43]

In spite of all the legal rights provided to the Muslim women under Muslim law, a husband has an absolute and unlimited right to repudiate the marriage at will, but a Muslim wife has no such right. One finds the common practice of misusing the Quranic provision of talaq by Muslim husbands. Even though law provides a wife the right to divorce, in reality she continues in a position of legal inferiority and insecurity, as long as the husband's unilateral right to divorce continues to be recognized. Although theoretically, a divorced wife is entitled to provisions and maintenance, it often proves impossible in practice to collect the promised mehr. Women are too ignorant and in experienced to fight for their rights. Besides they are far more afraid of public opinion, and the very act of appearing in court is usually enough to put them beyond the pale of respectability, since that is considered as coming out of purdah.[44]

Moreover with regard to divorce, because of the patriarchal structure of society, religious injunctions are interpreted in such a manner as to benefit men only. Even though under Islamic law, a man cannot torture his wife, poor women are vulnerable to harassment and abuse. Laws are enforced by the Ulema, but laws are violated. Some women do seek legal redress from Anzuman an Islamic court, but generally they abstain. The Maulvis take charge of disciplining and advising youth according to the precepts of law and religion.

A vast majority of Muslim women do not possess the freedom to choose their own life partner, to divorce, or to remarry. Polyandry, even though it exists, is not very widespread, and usually a second wife is taken only after divorce from the first wife. Qazis are appointed for judicial works. Although girls inherit their mother's property, and have rights over their dowry, in practice, women exercise little or no control, and their dowry is used for common family purposes. Even when a man marries for the second time, respect and status has to be accorded to the first wife. The second wife enjoys great respect, and is sometimes in a better position than the first wife.

Unwanted pregnancies out of wedlock contravene the Holy law, but women in general have no freedom in the exercise of reproductive choices. Unwanted pregnancies are prevented by discouraging free mixing of eligible young men and women, and strictly abiding by family restrictions and the Holy law. Moreover, as most marriages are arranged there are few opportunities for children to be born out of wedlock.

Syed Ahmed quoting Saiyidan Hammed concluded: "The fact of the matter is that we Muslims selectively practice whatever suits our needs. We indulge in triple talaq, in polygamy, in dodging mehr and maintenance. We ascribe our actions to our religious sanctions, and continuously harp on our religious code. But we blatantly, violate the injunctions of Islam. We pronounce triple talaq without following the commands pertaining to it. We marry again and again without adhering to the commands pertaining to the second subsequent marriage. Thanks to the way we practice it, Islam is looked upon by the world as the most anti-gender religion. For this perception, it is we Muslims who are to be blamed. It is time we applied the corrective to our own selves and stop using religion as an excuse for our misdemeanours".[45]

Women are also required to make the Haj, but financial constraints and poor health, have resulted in only a very few Muslim women from Manipur making the pilgrimage. Widows are barred from the Haj. Similarly, although there is no legal injunction prohibiting women's entry into places of worship, women are not seen praying in a mosque. In exceptional cases, when invocations have to be offered to stave off illness, misfortune, older women enter the mosque to pray (but not when males are inside).

References

1. M.A. Rahman, The Culture of Manipuri Muslims (Pangals), p. 40.

2. Md. Riyazuddin Chaudhury – Muslim Contribution to the Culture of Manipur, pp. 41-42.

3. Md. Riyaz Ahmed Shah – Status of Muslim Women in Manipur State, p.1.

4. Md. Ahmad Ali Shah op.cit. p.79 cit. M.A. Janab Khan 'Manipur Muslim', Imphal 1972., pp. 37-38.

5. Abdus Sahid Chowdhury – Souveniur IV – The Meitei Pangal – Socio Cultural Highlights.

6. Ibid.

7. Syed Ahmed – Muslims in Manipur: Quest for an identity, p. 8.

8. Ibid., p. 7.

9. M.A. Rahman op.cit, pp. 42-43.

10. A. Rahman – The Culture of Manipuri Muslim (Pangals) and Meitei Influences, p. 6.

11. A. Hakim Shah – The Role of Pangals (Manipuri Muslims) in Games and Sports in Manipur.

12. Salam Irene – Advent of Islam and Institutional structures and practices in Manipur, cit, Monica Dufft toft – Getting religion – The Puzzling case of Islam and Civil war, p. 124.

13. E.W. Dun – Gazetter of Manipur, Delhi 1979, p. 16.

14. Mc Culloch – Account of the Valley of Manipur (Reprint 1980), pp. 14-15.

15. Mh. Ahmad Ali Shah op.cit, p. 31.

16. Kheiruddin Khullakpam – Turko Afghan Chada Naoda Circles, Lilong, Manipur 1949.

17. O. Bhogeshor and Janab Khan – Nongsamei, Imphal 1973, p. 77.

18. Report on Socio-Economic Survey of Meitei Pangal, op.cit, p. 8.

19. Ibid., p. 30.

20. Salam Irene op.cit P. 3. Cit. Richard M. Eaton op.cit., p. 230.

21. Syed Ahmed, op.cit., pp. 3-4.

22. Salam Irene – Manipur Muslim Women, p. 42 cit. Syed Ahmed – Status of Muslim women in Manipur, p. 56.

23. Salam Irene – Advent of Islam op.cit., p. 4.

24. Syed Ahmed – Muslims in Manipur op.cit., p. 6.

25. Salam Irene – Advent of Islam op.cit., p. 4.

26. Ibid cit. Syed Ahmed op.cit, p. 9.

27. Ibid., p. 4.

28. Mh. Ahmad Ali Shah op.cit., pp. 31-32.

29. Ibid., p. 33.

30. Syed Ahmed op.cit., pp. 1, 7, 8.

31. Ibid.

32. Mh. Ahmed Ali Shah op.cit. p. 37.

33. Syed Ahmed op.cit., p. 10.

34. Salam Irene – Manipur Muslim Women's, p. 47.

35. K. Kunjani Devi –Muslim Women's Status in the Family and Society in Manipur, pp. 13-14.

36. A Qaiyum – (Advocate – Gauhati High Court) Misuse of Muslim personal law in Manipur Dec. 1994.

37. Manu Bhaskar – Family law and Customary Practices of Muslims p. 6. The Eastern Anthropologist, Vol. 49, No.1.

38. Md. Ahmad Ali. Shah op.cit., pp. 82-83.

39. S.A Akbar Abadi: Islamic Law in Modern Times-Published in Islam and Comparitive Law, Quarterly, Vol. 1. No. 3 (N. Delhi) 1981, pp. 201-202, ed. T. Mahmood.

40. M.N. Srinivas – India Social Structure, Sterling, Delhi 1980, pp. 74-75.

41. Manu Bhaskar, op.cit., p. 7.

42. A Hakim Shah Khullakpam op.cit, pp. 62-63.

43. Syed Ahmed Status of Muslim Women in Manipur, p. 57.

44. Salam Irene – Manipur Muslim Women, p. 46.

45. The Times of India, 15th Nov. 2001.

5

Administration Governance, Political Participation

A Rahman quoting from Musalman-e-Manipuri written in Urdu by Maulana Rahim-Uddin, and edited by Azizur Rahman and Shariat-ullah Choudhury, wrote : three Muslims named Shaikh Ruba, Gora Khan and Ashique Shah came to Manipur from Rajbari (Pratapgarh Rajabari), and they settled in Manipur with royal permission. The Pangals in Manipur were governed by the Meidingngu, and had to perform lallup and work in the military organization. When the Cacharis attacked Manipur in 1604 A.D. the Pangals as Manipuri soldiers fought under king Khagemba (1597-1652) A.D. Pala Koireng was one of the Pangal Manipuri soldiers. In 1606, King Khagemba captured one thousand Pangals including Phanleitao, Maika, Tao, Sana Puthi, Tekka Raja (Dacca Raja), Keirungba, and Ponchengkha, and seventeen military officers including Muhammad Sani.

They were all employed by the king, and assigned various duties. The 'Khagemba Khunthok' was the largest immigration and settlement of the Pangals in Manipur.[1]

After the Mughals arrived in Cachar through Matak, they sent one Kabui Ahom to Khagemba extending friendship, and a proposal of marriage of a virgin (as Apanbi) to King Khagemba. But the latter not trusting the Mughals, made arrangements to protect himself near the Guwai river in the engagement that followed, King Khagemba captured three Mughal soldiers viz. Meeron Khan, Anankha and Mangkankha (according to Khagemba Langjei) or Amankha, Patan Kha and Mangkankha (according to Sana Mahee Laihui). They were subsequently employed in the royal garden of king Khagemba.[2]

Historical references (e.g. Puya 'Leithak Leikharol') of establishment of Pathan and Pasha Ningthourol in Manipur would indicate Muslim principalities or chieftainship. Meiteis have a seven clan set-up and four panna system, but muslims had no such system T.C. Hodson noted that the Muhammadans are distinct from the Meithei as is reasonable to expect, R. Brown stated that Muslims 'performed lallup as Manipuris', for ten days out of every forty days, except women. B.C. Allen described Lamjel (Lamchel) – A annual long distance race conducted with state patronage. "This Lamchel is a competition between the different 'Pannah' or classes among Manipuri population. The Brahmans, as also the lowest class of Manipuris, the Lois, are not allowed to compete, but Mussalmans may". A special Panchayat court also sits at Lilong for the trial of cases between Muhammadan Manipuris. L. Iboongohal Singh note, 'The Manipuri Mahomedans are governed by the Mahomedan law, except Khainaba, Chakthak and Nupimammal.[3]

King Khagemba was an administrative innovator. Departments or Loisangs were re-organised by him. He established a separate department for the Muslims-Pangan Shanglen.[4] The Muslims had separate administrative or government departments. "The next group of departments is in charge of affairs relating to the Panggans of Muhammad inhabitants, and consists of Panggan Sanglen, Panggan Inkhol, Panggan Sinha Loishang, Panggan Phundrei Loisnag, Panggan Kumar, Panggan Mall, Panggan Likli. The principal officer here is the Qazi.[5] The Pangal Loisnag was instituted by king Khagemba in the year 1606. In 1609, Shyed Ambia, Shyed Abdullah and Khalka Hussain came to Manipur, and they enlarged the Pangal Loisang by sub-dividing it into three : viz religious, social and judicial departments.[6]

The King was the absolute head of the state but generally ten ministers assisted him in administration. These ministers were known as Ningthou Pongba Tara. The king appointed the Muslim Muhamed Shahni as one of the 'Pongba Tara'.[7] He was the first Muslim minister to be so appointed.

The Panggan Sanglen as its name implied was the department in charge of looking after the king's horses and elephants. This entailed provision of suitable fodder to the animals and many persons were employed to collect fodder and supply it to the animals. The Panggan Ingkhol supervised those Muslims engaged in cultivation and gardening, Muslims had great expertise in growing tobacco (hidakmana). Tobacco leaf was becoming popular with the royal family as also the people. Special gardens at Ningthen Inkhol, khumidok Heinoukhong-nembi, keikhong Ingkhol etc. were assigned to them. Panggan Singa Loishang was the music department. A new kind of clarinet 'Singa' (Bangoon) was introduced by the Muslims, and the king and people were partial to it. The department also included drummers, singers and dancers. However, the clarinet players were favoured by the king 'they played the clarinet which pleased the king greatly'.[8] Panggan phundrei was the department supervising artisans like blacksmiths and carpenters who manufactured weapons and furniture, and also aided in construction of houses and bridges. Because of their proficiency, some Muslims were employed as royal artisans to work on engravings and decorations on furniture, palanquins, and the royal canopy.[9] Panggan Kumar was the pottery department. The Muslims had introduced the wheeling technique which enabled improvements and a refinement in pottery-pottery was an item of export from Manipur. Panggan Mall or the entertainment department employed acrobats and performers. Prior to the Muslim advent, such forms of entertainment were unknown, but they soon grew popular and won applause. Panggan Likli, supervised trade and commerce, especially in necklaces (lik) and chains, imported by the Muslims who were fluent in many Indian languages and so better able to assist in trade and commercial activities.[10] There was regular trade with Cachar. Three Pangals, Chuki Meihaiba, Huipuba and Singga Khongba who worked in the Pangal mall and the Singga Loishang of Manipur, visited Tripura in 1676. Mughal horses arrived in the capital of Manipur in April 1671.[11]

Some Muslims from Cachar and Sylhet and the Meitei Pangal joined as sepoys in the Manipur Levy of 1824. Shaikh Lobah Shaikh Shubah, Shaikh Chybah, Shaikh Prem (Jamai Mia), Shaikh Brow and Shaikh Seba from Cachar and Sylhet who joined the Manipur Levy settled in Manipur after the Anglo-Burmese war of 1826.

With the opening of the office of the Political Agent in 1835, some Pathans opted to live in Manipur as British India subjects with the permission of the Government of Manipur. Most were workers and soldiers of the British, some few were businessmen. When Manipur merged with the Indian Union, their descendants (Pathan Kora) remained in Manipur. Parumiya (Faruk Mia) Choudhury ran a business and served King Nar Singh who rewarded him for his services in 1845. Sunamiya Choudhury was a prominent businessman who extended his help to the people when there was scarcity of rice in 1896 at the Khwairamband Bazar at Imphal.[12]

The Meidingngu was the head of Government and ruled through the Darbar and administrative departments. The Darbar combined the powers of executive, judiciary and legislature; administrative departments comprised state and community departments. Their functioning covered all communities, including the Meitei-Pangal. Qualified persons among the latter were appointed to posts in the state departments. For the Meitei Pangal king Khagemba established the Mangkanshang a community department, Mohamed Sani was the Qazi and the Shanglakpa, and attended the Darbar. Immigration of Muslims was overseen by the Nongthonba (Finance Minister), who was the overseer of the Mangkanshang and the Pangal Shanglen. Between the years 1940-1943 Muhammad Waliullah was a member of Darbar and Maulvi Basir-uddin Ahmed (Base Lakpa) was a member of the darbar or interim Council in 1947. The darbar dealt with the heads of departments, revenue, education, police, jail, medical, public works, etc. Funds and expenditures were passed by it subject to the approval of the Governor of Assam. The Governor had original and appellate jurisdiction in civil and criminal cases. It covered the Pangal Panchayat too.

The Sana konung Manung Loishang (Palace Loishang) under the Pukharanba primarily catered to the needs of the king, Queen and palace. It comprised the following officers – (a) Keirungba Yarekshang (b) Leima Senba (c) Humairoi (d) Chong (e) Barber (f) Washerman, (g) Meitanshang (h) Arangba (i) Anamshang (j) office of godowns (k) Keirungba Maroi (l) Keibijila (m) office of Pena (n) Shamjilloi (o) Kitna (p) Malli (q) Panji Loishang and (r) Tanyeishang. In the Keirungba Yarekshang, a Meitei pangal could serve as yarekpa in the military store, for e.g. Pangal Haoba was a Yarekpa sepoy in 1860. He and Jagat Singh were given capital punishment at Shugnu for stealing of guns from the military store. The Keirungba Yarekshang arranged for the requirements of the king, through a number of officers in charge of different works of supply. When the king toured villages, he oversaw the arrangements (provision of carpets, bedding, linen etc.)

The Leimasenba attended upon the Queen and Princess, and provided services and goods required by them. A pheida (eunch) looked after the tribute from the Pangal Ingkhol, situated at Lakhong. There was a Piba of the Meitei-Pangal Leima-Shija Phambalnai of Khabam Pana, who was appointed Yellangba, collector of vegetables, cereals, grain, jute etc. produced by the Pangal Ingkhol. He was not exempt from lallup. Laiba, grandson of Mohammad Sani was the Leima-Shija Phambalnai during the reign of king Charairongba. During the reign of king Chingthangkhomba, Cheksha (Zaid Shah) of the lineage of Mohammad Sani, held the post.

The Humairoi was a department of bamboo handicrafts. Some of its attendants were used for the service of fanning the king, inclusive of Meitei-pangals. They also assisted the Chongkhanba in carrying the Sana Sekpin or royal umbrella over the king. The Anamshang office of Seal and Posts employed some Meitei-Pangals to carry important messages, e.g. Khamba Muhammad during Khagembas reign, Syed Siliman (Suleiman), Silim Khan in Khunjaoba's reign. Muslims were also employed in the Tanyeishang which announced the hour in the palace, and performed services of drumming when necessary. Some Meitei Pangals served as samnat pung-yeibas, nagna pungyeibas and tomal pungyeibas. There were also Muslim buglers in the king's army who were employed as sentries both day and night. Pibas (eldest son) in the kingdom belonged to the Ningthousenba Loishang, introduced by king Naophangba. Under the Pheida Hanjaba, Meitei Pangals served as personal attendants to the King and Princess. Story telling (wari-leeba) and singing (eeshei shakpa) occurred at night, and Muslims too were employed they performed the Janginamah or Jang-i-Namah. The story tellers spoke of the kings achievements in administration and in war. The Jangi Namah continued to be performed in the reings of king Churachand Singh (1891-1941) and King Budhachandra. The Janginamah had two story-tellers, one read in a sweet voice the Janginamah script in Urdu, written by a scholar or Maulvi, and the other translated it into Meiteilon. The stories covered the entire range of human emotions, patriotism bravery, war, peace, pardon, etc. renowned story tellers were 'Basheimayum Asad ullah (Asatullah) Maulvi of Khergao, and Korimayum Moonshi (Kori Moonshi) of Kairang in the 1930's and the early 1940s, they were joined by Ipham Tonjao of Khetri Iril Mapal, Ipham Rajak Ali (Rajali) of Khetri Iril Mapal, and Muhammad Gulabsing in the 1940's Janginamah was popular in Muslim villages too upto the 1950s. The story tellers did not belong to the Loishang but their performances were arranged by the Ningthousenba Loishang. The Lalmi Loishang was the war department. All Manipuri subjects could become soldiers and had to render lallup. In Manipur, a number of Meitei-Pangals served as Sepoys-Pangals Siphai. Some were attached to the king's army and worked in the palace-others were posted to villages. They acted both as warriors and couriers conveying important dispatches, and were supervised in their work by the Senapati. In peace times, they maintained law and order, prevented theft, as also attacks by wild tigers. The king appointed a Pangal-Manjor also known as Pangal Bengoon Manjor in the Lalmi Loishang. Before the seven years devestation, there was also a Lanjingba or Lanchingba from the Meitei Pangals in the Lalmi

Loishang. Mohammad Sani was a Lanchingba in King Khagemba's reign, and Ngangba in King Bhaigya Chandra's reign. The Qazi, who was ranked as a Lalchingba or major, was a military-cum-civil officer who worked under the supervision of the Senapati, and the Nongthonba, in the state. He supervised the Pangal soldiers, and the Qazi of Mangkanshang acted as a commander in war under the king when necessary.

The Qazi was ranked as Qazi-ul-Qazat (chief judge) in the Mangkanshang and Pangal Shanglen, based on shariat law. But he was also a military officer Lanchingba, and Shingga Loi Shang and Pangal Shanglen were attached to the King's army. The buglers and drummers were assigned to the first and performed duties as soldiers. The Pangal Shanglen community department regulated the affairs of the Meitei-Pangals till 1791. Those Meitei Pangals who worked in the magazine as sentries, were also soldiers of Lalmi Loishang. Meitei pangal soldiers like other Manipuri soldiers wore a black dhoti upto the knee, a red jacket and a white turban. The Meitei Pangal Shagol Makok and syce of Mangkanshang and Pangal Shanglen, formed part of the cavalry. Under the Samuhanjaba, some Meitei Pangals participated in hunting, and assisting officials in training elephants in the shong (enclosure for elephants).[13]

The Meitei Pangals played an important role in defending the territorial integrity of the Manipur kingdom from the seventeenth century onwards. They were in fact, vital in defence and war. They had close ties with the Meiteis, and were moreover, 'possessed of an open, liberal character, unlike their co-religionist in other parts of the world.[14] A wedge drew the communities apart after the adoption of Vaishnavism by the Meiteis, and their subsequent treatment of Muslims as being of lower status. In the early part of their settlement, Kheiruddin Khullakpam states, that they had a major role to play in the protection of border areas in the eastern and southern sections of the Kingdom. Many Forts were constructed for defense and placed under the command of Pangal Officers for e.g. Phundrei, Heirok, Ushangkhong, Malom Khongnangband, Changamdabi Kangla, Ukok Mayang Imphal and Pangal Tabi.[15]

To the fortress at Heirok Wangmayum Sagei was appointed as commandant, likewise, at the fortresses at Ukhongsang, Changamdabi Kangla Ulok, Mayang Imphal, Pangal Tabi and Malom Khongangband; the troops were led by Phusam Sagei, Sajoubam, Ipham Mayum and two sageis viz, Khullakpam and Makak Mayum. Another fortress was placed under Ibrahim Miya in Thoubal, to check raids of hostile tribals, in Khagemba's reign. The descendants of Ibrahim Miya are still residing at Thoubal Moijing. The fortress was placed under Shaikh Salimullah at Yairipok, and Muslims were urged to settle there.[16] Meitei Pangals of the Aribam clan like Pala Koireng and Khungam fought the war of 1604 as Manipuri soldier's agains the Cacharis. Muhammad Sani Say as Lalchingba (Major) and other Meitei Pangal Soldiers were appointed by King Khagemba to fight the Shan principalities in 1614. During the reign of Chingthangkhomba or Jai Singh the Lanchingba of the Pangal Shanglen was put under the

Senapati, whereas the military service of Mangkan Shang and the Pangal Shanglen was under the Lalmi Loishang upto the 1830's. In 1702, King Charairongba put to death Syed or Merai Ngangba, the Qazi-ul-Qazat of the Mangkanshang and Pangal Shakom (Shah Kusum), Naoshamcha Pukhramba, Angom Lanhang and Pangal Hongba for joining the revolt of Ibungo Loiyumba, brother of the king. They were tried in the Top Garod, presided over by the Senapati.[17]

In 1679, during the reign of Paikhomba, some Muslims were sent to Keinou to protect it against the marauding raids of wild animals. Placed under the command of Ukhan Tollotma, they were made to settle there by the king's order.[18] This indicates that the Muslims played a part not only in military affairs, but in defence against wild animals through colonization of an area.

On 14 Ingga (probably june) 1721, Meitei Pangal soldiers under the command of Haobam Pukhranba fought against a threat from Shomsok, a Shan principality, they were victorious and returned with sixty seven Shan captives. There were Burmese invasions in 1722 and 1723. In the fight against them Pangal Shanglakpa (Khullakpam Ngouba), with thirty buglers fought for the Manipuri king. Some of the prominent Muslim soldiers in this battle at Wangjing were Makakmayum Khungam, Makakmayum Mooba, Khullakpam Ngouba, Thouba Makakmayum, Basheimayum Khungam Longjam Aroi, Longjam Laphong, Pathanmayum Chabrullah (Zabbar-ullah). In the revolt of 1755 of Tonlen Tonba, son of Garibniwaz against Maramba, some Meitei Pangals were killed. And in King Maramba's reign, some Meitei Pangals along with other Manipuris were captured by the Burmese. So also, in 1755 and 1758 when Alaungpaya invaded Manipur and in 1769-1770 when Hsin invaded. In the revolt of Marjit against his brother king Chourajit, a Meitei Pangal of the Maibam clan of Khabam Pana lost his life. During the seven years devestation (1891-1826) the Bugyidaw's armies captured many Meitei Pangals. As described by Robert Brown – 'with all the other sections of the Manipuri community the greater portion of the Meitei Pangal was carried into captivity by these ruthless invaders. The captives were mainly from the Khabam Pana.[19]

By 1825, King Gambhir Singh had formed the Manipur Levy with the help of the British. There were sixteen Meitei Pangal soldiers in it. They were (1) Shaik Sanaullah (2) Shaik Rifye (3) Shaik Soobul (4) Refy Mohumed (5) Lool Mohumed (6) Barkootodah (7) Loll Muumud (8) Mohumed Nazir (9) Shaikh Shubah (10) Shaik Seba (11) Shaik Prem (on command) (12) Shaik Brow (13) Shaik Lobah (14) Shaik Chybah (15) Shaik Khambah and (16) Shaik Sayja. Barkootoolah alias Tolen-Ipham who fought the Burmese as a part of the Manipur Levy, was appointed as the Qazi in the Pangal Shanglen by King Gambhir Singh. He was popularly known as Tolen Qazi by the Manipuris. He was entitled to 'Mana lou' and allowed to use one paat (lake) during his lifetime. The paat was named 'Qazi paat' by the king. It was situated on the northern Kiyamgei near Takhok.

When king Nara Singh ascended the throne in 1844, he permitted the Meitei Pangal soldiers to work in the

Lalmi Loishang. In a revolt by three brothers in 1850, some Pangals lost their lives. A Pangal Manjor Mohammad Nizam Ipham of Khetri Bengoon was assaulted by a Pathan soldier in 1852 at Kangla. In the rebellion of Jugindro, younger brother of King Surchandra Singh (1886-1889), two Meitei Pangals died in 1887. Some of the Meitei Pangals who served under the Lalmi Loishang were Koushali (Kousar Ali) Lallupchingba, Tolando Basheimayum, and Shanggai Makakmayum, all subedars; Pheira Thongkhongmayum – an amandar, Sher Shah Makakmayum and Khela Makakmayum – Kuts, Angou Makakmayum – havildar, Ajijur Rahman Ipham – Shagol Makok, Moni Ipham – Bengoon Amandar, Niyamat –Ullah Ipham, Melei Singgakhongbam, Qarim-buglers, Babu Ipham, Chouba Singga – Khongbam, Hamoon Ipham, Naokan Tomba, Khanba Ipham, Khema Ipham Chaodonpa, Sanaullah Nonjainayum, Khoya Shah Makakmayum, Tonjao, Joy Jatra, Angou Makakmayum, Roopa Mia Phundreimayum, Rahmatullah Makakmayum, Kena Makamayum, Chaobi Haider, Tonjao Khullakpam, Khamba Ipham,[20] Kousali Ipham was in charge of the Lallupchingba of the Meitei Pangal. Bengoon Khongba (buglers) continued to serve in the army and resided in quarters at the western kangla gate. The duty of the buglers was specially significant in the night hours – Yusuf Ali Makakmayum was one of the sentries posted at the western gate of Kangla.[21] In March 1891, the British entered Dasu Sardar's residence and his wife, A Meitei pangal from Thoubal Moijing, had her ears and fingers cut off. B. Kullachandra and Badaruddin have given a list of Pangal soldiers who fought in the Anglo-Manipur war of 1891. It differs from the list of those who worked in the Lalmi Loishang. The names of these soldiers were collected by the Manipuri Muslim Historical Society. They were:

(1) Babu Alias Sangdrokpa, Sagei Ipham of Kairang Ipham Leikai, who after the war was a member of the Muslim panchayat for about forty years.

(2) Singa Diwan of Kairangkhabeisoi who fought under the command of Paona Brajabasi.

(3) Niyam Attullah, Sagei Ipham of Khetri Awang leikai, accompanied Paona Brajabasi, was wounded and subsequently died.

(4) Moni Amandar, Sagei Ipham of Khetri Awang Leikai

(5) Hamoon, younger brother of Moni Amandar.

(6) Naokan Tomba, Sagei Ipham.

(7) Ajijur Rahman (Shamu), Sagei Ipham was a cavalry leader who was injured by a bullet, but recovered and fought in the Khongjom war.

(8) Khamba (Irong Tomba) Sagei Ipham of Keirao fought against the Silchar column in the 1891 war.

(9) Khamba of Keirao.

(10) Chaodonpa of Kiyamgei who died on the Khongjom battle field.

(11) Sanaola Haji, Sagei Nongjaimamum of Keikhu who was injured.

(12) Sher Shah (Chibandokut), Sagei Makakmayum of Lilong Leihaokhong succumbed to a bullet injury at Pallel.

(13) Koya Singh, Sagei Makakmayum, elder brother of Sher Shah.

(14) Yusey Ali, younger brother of Sher Shah posted as palace guard at Kangla.

(15) Khel Kut, Sagei Makakmayum of Lilong.

(16) Tonjao, Sagei Makakmayum.

(17) Lamboiba Habildar, Sagei Makakmayum of Lilong.

(18) Talandon Subedar, Sagei Bhagi Mayum of Lilong.

(19) Pheira Jamandar, Sagei Thongkhon Mayum of Lilong.

(20) Sangai Subedar, Sagei Makakmayum Angouba.

(21) Jay Jatra, Sagei Makak Angouba of Lilong.

(22) Angou, younger brother of Jay Jatra.

(23) Malei Bugler, Sagai Singa Khongbam of Lilong.

(24) Abdul Karim Bugler, Sagei Merai Mayum of Lilong.

(25) Asgqar Ali (Rupo Ali Mia) Sagei Phondrei Mayum of Sangai Yumpham was a follower of Paona Brajabasi.

(26) Rahamatullah (Oraoba), Sagei Makakmayum of Yairipok Tulihal.

(27) Umo Nongsaibam, Sagei Nongshaibam.

(28) Haji Abungton, Sagei Khullakpam of Yairipok, Tulihal.

(29) Sadhu, Sagei Makak Angouba of Yairipok.

(30) Yusuf (Kona) Sagei Makak Mayum.

One Muslim Chaobi Haidar was exiled to the Andaman Islands for taking an active part in the war against the British.[22]

It is thus evident, that the Meitei Pangals were actively associated with the Lalmi Loishang, and took an active part in warfare.

The Cheirap – The King of Manipur was the head of the judiciary which comprised the Cheirap, the Kuchu, the Paja (Pacha) and other subsidiary courts like the Mangkanshang the Pangal Shanglen, the Pangal Panchayat, Brahma Saba etc. criminal justice in respect of the Meitei Pangal was administered by the Cheirap which tried adultery cases too. The guilty woman was punished through khunggoinaba and fining (phouba) Capital punishment was also the prerogative of the Cheirap. Religious cases of the Pangals were adjudjed by the Mangkashang of the Pangal Shanglen, and by the Muslim Panchayat. Pangal sepoys or soldiers, of Lalmi Loishang, were tried in the Bijaygrod. Punishments included capital punishment, imprisonment, mutilation and exile.[23]

With respect to justice, the Kazi was the head who administered justice to the litigants in accordance with the provisions of Islamic law. He combined both judicial and executive powers. The first Kazi was appointed in the reign of king Khagemba and sat in the Pangal Shanglen. Different terms were used for the heads of the Pangal Loishang, viz. Kazi, Khullakpa and Kazi-ul-Quzat. A literate person was appointed as kazi, a person who was illiterate but possessed full knowledge of administration and judiciary was termed 'Khullakpa' (head of a village), and if two persons were appointed as kazi, the more qualified was titled kazi-ul-Quzat.[24] Appointment of such persons only serves to underline the necessity of judjing Muslims according to the provisions of the Quran and shairat. From Kheiruddin's list of kazis, it is clear that kazis were appointed from the time of Muslim settlement till the establishment of colonial rule. The list of Kazis as given in the 'Yadd-i-Kurshi-Nama' is as follows :

1. Kazi Muhmad Shani-1606 A.D.
2. Saikh Muhmad Chunet or Chunalia (Khullakpa) 1627 A.D.
3. Kazi Sayid Ambiya 1649 A.D.
4. Kazi Sayid Husain 1658 A.D.
5. Tomba Khullakpa 1676 A.D.
6. Kazi Sayid Suleiman 1679 A.D.
7. Ukatullah 1687 A.D.
8. Melei Ngangba Qazi – 1708 A.D.
9. Shiv Muhmad or Shangairakpa Thouba Taothongtaba 1713 A.D.
10. Mir Kazi Khunpuba – 1735 A.D.
11. Kazi Ismail or Gouranani 1747 A.D.
12. Ali Mullah Kazi – 1756 A.D.
13. Kulsum Kazi – 1793 A.D.
14. Narisrullah Ibne Rahmullah Makak Angouba – 1826 A.D.

15. Barqtullah or Tolel Kazi 1826 A.D.
16. Hera Kazi 1836 A.D.
17. Surba Kazi 1851 A.D.
18. Ali Miya Kazi 1878 A.D.
19. Ira Kazi 1889 A.D.

Among other Kazis only three attained the position of Kazi-ul-Quzat. They were (a) Kazi Muhmad Shani (b) Kazi Sayid Husain (c) Kazi Shiv Muhmad or Taothongtaba.[25] The establishment of a separate judiciary for the Muslims continued under colonial rule.

Some Meitei Pangals were also employed in the State military police service, known to the Muslims as 'Saheb Khanba' or 'Saheb Thaana'. The Imperial Regent introduced the chowkidari system on 18th Jan.1892. The chowkidar was appointed for every hundred houses. A chowkidar received Rs. 2/- per month, and half a pari (land unit) of rent free land, and twelve pots of paddy as salary. Many Meitei Pangals were appointed chowkidars, and performed the task of maintaining law and order in the villages, checking crime, and assisting the Muslim Panchayat. Crimes of theft, assault, murder, came under the jurisdiction of the Panchayat, and the chowkidar could detain a criminal with the approval of a Qazi. Although the chowkidar patrolled the village, he was not permitted to pry into the private life of the villagers. He was answerable to the panchayat, and reported weekly on matters pertaining to the village, such as epidemics, disease, state of cultivation, welfare of the inhabitants. He wore uniform when on duty, he was elected by the people but his post had to be confirmed by the Political Agent. He directed the villagers to repair valley roads, and collect supplies for officers on tour during the British rule. Chowkidars were assisted by nambors in the Muhallahs, and together they were responsible for meeting all requirements of officials on tour. Nambors enjoyed the Phoukhai, originally given to chowkidars for their services at night. As the chowkidars did not perform night duty, this allowance was made over to the nambors. In 1947, there were 248 chowkidars i.e. a ratio of 1 to 92,639 populations.[26]

In Meitei Pangal villages the Loupanaba was the first collector of rent of rice land or 'lou'. The Loumirakpa or Lourungba of the Meitei Pangal recorded it for state purposes. He kept all land records, names of men liable to perform lallup. The Loumirakpa with the help of the Loupanaba under the Qazi, held the Khundin of the lallup, in addition to revenue collection. The Loumirakpa was the lalchingba/shanglakpa of the Mangkanshang and Pangal Shanglen. There were many village Loupanabas, All matters relating to land, leaving it barren or cultivating it, were decided by them. The rent of the Phamlou i.e. lands given to officials was supervised by the Phourungba. The land measurement system was equally applicable to land of the Muslim i.e. two loushen = 1 tong, 2 tong = 1 loukhai, 2 loukhai=1 sangam, 2 sangam= 1 lourak, 2 lourak=1 pari, A pari was approximately two and a half acres.

Some Muslims from outside Manipur were engaged to work in the revenue department. Maulvi Faizuddin Ahmed of Jorhat served as Sub-Deputy Collector from 28th December 1905, upto 1909 and as Deputy Collector

1909-1911. Maulvi Abdul Wahid of Cachar was Sub-Deputy Collector from 15th October 1909- he returned to his native place in 1917. Amanullah khutheibam of Keikhu, Imphal was a Kanungo during the reign of Maharajah Chandrakirti Singh. Some Muslims were appointed as Amins. Mohammad Basiruddin Ahmed Khullakpam (Bashelakpa) of Khergao, Imphal was appointed as Laipham Lakpa in 1945 and as Tahsildar in the following year. Meitei Pangals paid house tax; they had 305 houses in Imphal with a population of 1525. Robert Brown had recorded the number of Meitei pangals in the countryside in 1873. The census of 1901 put the population of the valley at 1, 80,960 but the population of the Meitei pangals and the number of their habitations was no recorded. In the time of the Imperial Regent, one Maulvi Faizuddin Ahmed was sub-deputy collector in charge of land revenue, and in 1909-1910, Maulavi Abdul Wahid held the post. In 1807, one Sanasaba Pangal worked as Unamlakpa (forest officer) in 1807.[27]

The people of the kingdom were divided into different panas. T.C. Hodson asserted that the pana was personal and not territorial. "This population is composed of different communities including the Mussalman. The Pana Loishang in each pana had two departments' viz. the Shanglen (main department) and Shangkhuba (subordinate department). During the British rule the pana became a land revenue division. The panas ensured the efficient working of the lallup. The Lallupchingba was the intermediary between the state officials at the capital. And the men in the villages. Mohamad Sani was appointed Lalchingba of the Meitei

Pangals in 1610, and Ngangba, his grandson, during the reign of king Chingthangkhomba or Bhagyachandra.[28]

Lallup implied performing service for the state for ten days out of every forty. If a man abstained from lallup, he was fined one rupee; even if he was sick, he had to provide a substitute. The effect of the lallup was the division of Meitei Pangals into two groups – the Khuncha and the Ingkhol Shangba.

The Khuncha comprised singgakhongbas and buglers, who served in the Lalmi Loishang, the Pangal Siphai of the villages, and the officers of Mangkangshang and Pangal Shanglen. Not many Muslims had settled in the khabam and laipham panas. These Muslims enjoyed a superior status because of the political, military and administrative duties that they performed. The defended the state against aggression, performed the duties of village guards, and as couriers to pass on important messages, protected against wild animals. (By signaling danger through blowing of the bugle/ trumpet).

The ingkhol shangba literally meant those who worked on and looked after homesteads, but for the Muslims it included those proficient in trades like carpentry, turning, pottery, blacksmiths (known for manufacture of thangshang Tha-shaba-sword) goldsmiths (Pangal Sanashaba known for making nasika – nose ring, and nari phabi lei (ear ring) acrobats, bottle-makers, fishermen. They too had to perform lallup and Robert Brown remarks. 'The Meitei Pangals performed lallup as Manipuris, and had the reputation of being an honest and hard working class. In return for their service, they enjoyed one pari of land on rent. The Muslims had to also supply vegatables, fruits, cereals, corn to the king, as and when necessary'.

A department known as Mangkanshang, and subsequently the Pangal Shanglen looked after the welfare of the Meitei Pangals in the Manipur kingdom. The first was created in 1606, 'mangkan' or 'mangal' is a corrupt form of 'Mughal' and 'shang' meant office. The Mughals were known as mangkhan by the Manpuris, and the Muslims who migrated from the west, particularly Bengal in the seventeenth upto the first half of the eighteenth century in Manipur were officially known as 'Mangkan; though they may have been Turks, Mongols, Pathans, Afghans, Bengali Muslims. The Muslim migrants were termed as 'Pangals' they are identical with the Mankan who immigrated and settled in the kingdom of Manipur. The Mangkan Shang was situated just near the south of the Nonghum Shang in the Kangla. It was accidentally burnt in 1690, again in 1692, and November 1724. In 1730, it was rebuilt at the same site. The department performed political, social, economic, judicial and military duties.[29]

The Qazi was the principal officer; he was assisted by two Khunglois (attendants) and given five paris of land rent free-loucha. King Khagemba made Mohamad Sani Qazi-ul-Qazat-he was also known as the 'Mangkan Ningthou Sani' or 'Muhammatani', or Mohamad Sani or Prashenna Lalchinglen. After the Syeds who were well-versed in Isllamic law arrived in 1608, Syed Ambiya was made the Qazi of the Mangkan Shang, enjoying civil and criminal jurisdiction. He gave his judgement in accordance with the shariat, and was well-versed in

Muslim personal law. The Qazi sat on the Pharangji Phida, a decorated carpet placed on the Korphal or official chair. A special seat known as the 'Ningthourel Tangbal' was reserved in the court for the king. The Qazi, the Shanglakpa, Dolaipaba and Diwan of the Mangkan Shang were all attached to the Lalmi Loishang. The Qazi had the responsibility of supplying Thoug Alloi (attendants) from among the Meitei-Pangals to serve the king, and perform duties in the palace (sanakonung) they were employed to fan the king and queen (humairoy), to hold the royal umbrella, to serve pan (kwasen) to fold the king's dhoti, to guard the granary (kei), to work as sentries, vetinary doctors, syces, huiroi, scouts for hunting, elephant riders, suppliers of elephant and Mangkan horse.

The Mangkan Shang had a Lakpa-Shanglakpa to supervise its five departments. They were (1) Pangal Ingkhol (2) Pangal Singga Loishang (3) Pangal Phundrei Loishang (4) Pangal Kumar and (5) Pangal Mall. There were also dolaipabas who policed Muslim settlements. Initially there was only one dolaipaba, later the number increased in proportion to the population.

The Mangkan Shang became the Pangal Shanglen in 1791 A.D. It was also known as the 'Khabam Shanglen', as most Meitei Pangals resided in the Khabam Pana. In addition to the five departments of the Mangkan shang, Pangal shanglen had a sixth department – Pangal Likli, It had officials such as the Qazi, Shanlakpa, Diwan, Dolaipabas and Yellangba, whose functions and powers were the same as the officers of the Mangkan shang. The last was a collector of vegetables and grain which were to be handed over to the Pheida for the king's use.

The Qazi remained the principal officer. Ali Mullah succeeded Mellei Meraimayum as Qazi, when the latter was dismissed in 1755, by King Maramba for supporting the rebellion of Prince Tollentomba. In 1791, Quslum Qazi was appointed, other duties continued to be performed as before. The Shanglakpa was a respected person-Maijou Khullakpam, a grandson of Mohamad Sani was the Shanglakpa in the Mangkan Shang and Mangalmayum Tonba a distinguished farmer, was Shanglakpa in the Pangal Shaglen in 1791, Habibullah Moijingmayum of Thoubal Moijing was the Shanglen lakpa in Marjit Singh's reign. Koushali (Koushar Ali) of Keirao Makting was the last Shanglen lakpa of the Pangal Shanglen which continued upto 1819.

The Pangals Ingkhol supplied the needs for vegetables, cereals etc. of the government. According to J.C. Higgins,the Meitei Pangals paid revenue in the form of dal, paper, jute, sugar. This is corroborated by R.K. Sanahal Singh. Although paper-making was known to the Meiteis before Sheikh Chunaid (Zunaid) arrived in Manipur, it received a spurt after his coming. The centre of production was Irong Chesaba, and the industry was patronized by the king, especially Maharajah Churachand. The paper produced had to be sold only to the king. And the workers were paid five paise per sheet of paper, although the market rate was ten paise in the 1940's. Raw materials required for manufacture like bamboo, jute, waste of sugarcane, were available in the Pangal Ingkhol especially Irong Chesaba. The Meitei Pangals used some paper for writing tawiz in Arabic and Urdu. The paper was supplied direct to the king.

Pangal Ingkhol was comprised of two parts – the Pangal Keikhongta and Pangal Ingkhol. Both specialized in the cultivation of certain crops and vegetables. Each Pangal Ingkhol grew sugarcane and produced red sugar (chuhi). The Yellangba collected the king's share and stored it in the granary at Lakhong. The Pangal Singga Loishang had civil and military responsibilities – its head was Singga Hanjaba, Sheikh Shani Mullah was the head in Khagemba's reign. Singga was a trumpet made of the horn of a buffalo or mithun and connected to a small bamboo of three to three and a half feet. It heralded movement and deployment in battle, and announced the king's arrival at Kangla; it was used in ritual ceremonies including funerals and cremations. The Pangal Singga Loishang was used to tame and train elephants, especially when they ran amuck. For e.g. the royal elephant 'Shamu Shenhongba' by Pathanmayum Qaanu of Shanggai yumpham – he was the singga khonga and was awarded the 'pajeng Phiran' by king Garibniwaz. The award was displayed recently in 1997 at the Manipur State Musuem. The department also included buglers who performed service for the palace and the military, known as Bengoon Khongba.

Pangal Phundrei Loishang – Manipur had two kinds of phundrei – Meitei and Pangal phundreis. Legs of wooden boxes and chairs shairuk were made by the latter, and wood was supplied by the Urungba. It also manufactured the stand or holder, and neck of the hookah, pe-moidon, a wooden polished cone for the top of the umbrella, phiran moidon, a wooden polished cone on top of the Manipur National Flag, saw, heedan (book-stand). All these items were handed over to the Nongthonba (Finance Minister), and kept in the

Lakhong. The first Pangal Phundreis were Kundan Khan and Zamaal Khan. A charge of one anna per rupee was levied on imports and exports of these items in the 1870's.

Pangal Kumar (derived from kumhar-potter) was the department for manufacturing phu (pots) for the state, using the wheeling technique. Nooriya Sheikh was the founder of the Pangal kumar (1607). It manufactured khum (drinking pot), Wuju khum (ablution pot) Pul (small pot for holding water), leirang (stove), yenkam (lampstand), phuhing (for deities), kharung (big water container), ngangoukhang (frying pan), chaphu and uyan (cooking pots), keghaam and wangkhum (bowls). The earthern ware pots were handed over to the Phurungba (store-keeper). These could be sold thereafter, to the public after the Nongthonba received the king's permission. The 'Pangalpul' or 'Irongpul' was popular for cooling water in summer, it had a smooth surface.

Pangal Mall – The department of acrobats and contortionists. Akun Shah and Kanba Shah were renowned for their feats. The Malls were later influenced by the 'Kabul Jagoi' of the Turko-Afghan and 'Kawali' – a special refined form of music of the nineteenth century, particularly in Chandra kirti's reign. The department performed 'Pousha Heiba (stick-fighting) it was done at the Mapal Kangjeibung, Imphal before king Chandrakirti. Performances continued into the first two decades of the twentieth century. T.C. Hodson remarked: 'The Mussalman section of the population contributes acrobats and contortionists, and there is always a troupe of low, sometimes, very low comedians, whose jests afford supreme delight to the crowd'. The Malls presented 'Mall Touba' in March 1912 at Mapal kangjeibung before King Churachand Singh and his guest, the king of Tripura. The Malls were a part of sports, games and cultural festivals.

Pangal Likli produced glass; production was started by some Muslims from Sylhet. It was a state run industry manufacturing bottles, phials, glass, looking glass, glass bangles. Because of increasing contact with the British, King Chandrakirti Singh established a glass factory in Manipur in the mid-nineteenth century. A levy of one anna per rupee was charged on looking glass. The Nongthonba remained the supervisor, and the state derived income from bottle production. Pangal Likli also made the Likli Taswi used by Meitei Pangals for religious purposes. The industry was adversely impacted by the Anglo-Manipur War of 1891, and it was not revived in the twentieth century. However, Mohammad Waliullah khut-heibam, a member of the Manipur State Darbar established a glass factory at Hafiz Hatta, Imphal in 1947.[30]

Meitei Pangal Villages – A village had three or four leikais. Several families constituted a leikai comprising a collection of houses, populated by persons of the same clan or yumnak. Goroh (from the Arabic Girawoh) was an organization of the same clan, containing a lup or club of constituent families in a defiend area 'Kollup', where the families were bound together in mutual assistance. Another organization 'Singlup' maintained the kabaristan and assisted in burial-arranging bamboos to be used in the tomb. It also conveyed news of a person's death, assisted the bereaved family with provisions and food supplies. There were two kinds of Kabaristans – that of one Singlup, and that of many clans.

The latter was known as Manglen (greater tomb estate). Its administrative functions also included assistance at nikah, sherni (feast) akikah (sacrifice of an animal).

Each khul (village) had a Muhallah attached to the Masjid. It is believed that the first mosque in the seventeenth century was built at Moirangkhom. A Muhallah initially meant a village, but as villages increased, Muhallah was an organization of the constitutent families of a Masjid. There were also Muhallahs of a leikai.

Men who lived in a village formed a leirup, which focused on lallup required for state developmental work in villages – such as construction and maintenance of roads bridges, embankments of rivers, digging of canals, streams. The khuncha in the village was made up of Pangal Siphais and Singga Khongbas, including bengoon khongbas, dolaipabas, huirois, keirungbas, loumirakpa, loupanaba.

It served as a village militia before the establishment of the Manipur levy. They were also deployed in war as for example in 1721, the Senapati Haobamcha Pukhranba led the Pangal Siphais, who invaded Shomsok, a principality of Ava, and captured 67 Burmese soldiers. Khunchas also caught tigers and were entrusted with the responsibility of ensuring security of life and property. A fine of Rs. 10/- was imposed if a tiger killed a cow within the village boundaries. Conversely, if a tiger was caught and tamed, the king rewarded the catcher (huirou) with Rs. 10/-. An interesting procedure was in practice to catch a tiger. The person who first learnt of tiger's presence burnt a 'tikki' (circular charcoal tablet) on a 'wai khudap' (cover of paddy), in a 'kegham' (earthern bowl), and passed it on to the neighbours, who is turn passed it on through the leikai and village. It was known as 'meihum chatpa'. Once encircled, the huiroy roared like a tiger. If there was a response from the tiger, dogs were sent to smell out the animal. They would retreat in fear from the spot, and the huiroys armed with 'lambu taa' (long spear) would kill the tiger.

Since a village was a primary unit of governance, a Khullakpa was appointed in Meitei-Pangal villages. He was the head or chief of the village. But his importance declined after the death of Mohammad Sani and the Shang Lakpa assumed his responsibilities. Some reforms took place in 1835, and the Qazi was relieved of military duties. But Pangal Manjor continued in the Lalmi Loishang. The Shanglakpa oversaw the lallup. Some Meitei Pangals were excused for instance, sons of the Qazi, Shanglakpa, Khullakpa, Loumirakpa, Imam, and winner of the race-'Khong Lamchel'. A meeting or 'Khundin' concerning lallup was held every nine days at the office of the Keirungba Yarekshang. Rules and regulations of lallup were not strictly enforced in June and October, as cultivators were busy with sowing, transplantation, reaping. If in an area, the men there were unable to complete the work given to them, they could enroll men from other areas, but this did not exempt the latter from the usual lallup service.

Muslim Panchayat – It was constituted in 1891-92 to try minor cases, and had five Muslim members who applied Muslim personal law to adjudication of civil cases. It functioned in the Qazi's guest house. A separate office building was inaugurated in Lilong on 4th February 1902. The political Agent and Superintendent of the state, Maxwell, appointed Mia Phundreimayum of Lilong as the Qazi of the Muslim Panchayat. Later the Qazi was appointed by the Maharajah. The Panchayat was assisted by chowkidars and village police in matters of arrest. The Panchayat sat twice a week, tried to dispose off cases amicably. In case of a dispute, where the subject matter was valued at less than Rs. 50/-, the case was tried by the Panchayat; otherwise it was referred to the Cheirap court. The only punishment was a fine of Rs. 50/-. Two civil Muharrirs and two criminal Muharrirs were attached to the panchayat. In the rules of the administration of justice and police 1891, it was provided that in any case, in which the complainant or plaintiff was a Muhammadan, and the accused or defendant a Hindu, the latter had the option of being tried by the Muslim Panchayat or the Panchayat near his home. It vice versa, the matter was tried by the Muhammadan Panchayat. If the accused were both Hindus and Mohammadans, the dispute went for trial to the Cheirap. The Panchayat, when it sat as a court, had three or five members, and the verdict of the majority was accepted, but it did not try cases where the personal interests of a member were involved. A member of the Panchayat received a pari of land rent free during his term of office, and an honorary title – Wayentouba.[31]

The Maharajah of Manipur constituted a Manipur State Constitution Making Committee on 12th December 1946 of fourteen members, which included Maulvi

Bashiruddin Ahmed. An Interim Council was formed on 15th August, 1947, with the lapse of British Paramountcy. In this council, Maulvi Bashiruddin Ahmed was made Minister of Medical, P.W.D. and Jails. A franchise sub-committee was formed in 1947 and Maulvi Bashiruddin Ahmed was the secretary. The valley was divided into 29 constituencies, and in three constituencies, where there were numerous Mohammadans, plural voting would be enfored i.e. one voter would have two votes, one for the Mohammadan, and the other for the non-Mohammadan. According to the Manipur State Constitution Act 1947, the state Assembly would comprise fifty-three members of which three seats would be for the Mohammadans. The Meitei Pangals were given the right to elect their members by ballot. The elections for the state assembly were held in March 1948, and five Meitei-pangals were elected, Muhammad Suleiman from Mayang Imphal, Muhammad Amjad Ali from Yairipok, and Muhammad Alimuddin from Lilong. The other two were Muhammad Abdul of Kiyamgei, and Maulvi Kadir Khan of Lilong. In the government headed by M.K. Priyabrata Singh, first Chief Minister of Manipur (1948), Muhammad Aliduddin was appointed Minister of Medical and Jail. The Manipur Merger Agreement came into force on 15th October 1949, and in January 1950, Manipur became a part-C state of the union of India. The Chief Commissioner of Manipur had an advisory Committee, and Mohammad Alimuddin was an honorary member. There was also, a Manipur Electoral College of thirty Elected Members in 1951 and Muhammad Tomba Mia and Muhammad Alimuddin were Elected Members.[32] Prior to the Merger of Manipur with India in 1949, an election was held to the First Manipur State Assembly. The First Manipur State Assembly was elected on Adult Franchise in July 1948. "The representatives returnable from General, Hill and Mohammedan constituencies were in the ratio of 30:18:3 respectively, with an Additional two seats for the Representatives of Educational and commercial interests. The whole valley of Manipur was divided into twenty-nine constituencies. Three of them were plural constituencies." The special constituencies from which one Muslim and one Hindu were returned were Lilong, Mayang Imhal and Yairipok.

The State Assembly was however dissolved after Manipur's merger with the Dominion Government of India on 15th of October 1949. Manipur became a part C State, and the state continued to be administered by the President through a Chief Commissioner or a Lieutant Governor, who acted as his agent. There was an Advisory Council appointed by the President in consultation with the Chief Commissioner. The Council met once in three months, presided over by the Chief Commissioner. The Council was an Advisory body, and as such, its advice was not necessarily binding on the Chief Commissioner. On November 1, 1956, Manipur became a Union Territory under the Union Territorial Council Act, 1956.

In the Electoral College of 1952 to 1957, only two Muslims took oath of office as members viz Muhammad Alimuddin from Lilong and Muhammad Tomba Mia from Lambi Keirao. Their term of office lasted from 14th February 1952 to 1st September 1957. There were only thirty constitutional members. At that time, the Muslim population comprised of 37,197 persons, So Elected members represented a fair percentage of the Muslim population. The Territorial Council consisting of thirty elected members and two nominated members was constituted on 16/8/1957. To this Territorial Council two Muslims were elected, once again Muhammad Alimuddin of Lilong, and also Mohammad Amjad Ali from Irilbung Yairipok. There were thirty four members of the Territorial Council in all.

The Territorial Council was later converted into the Territorial Legislative Assembly in June 1963. The Territorial Legislative Assembly consisting of thirty elected members and two nominated members started to function from 23/7/1963. In this Assembly Muslim population was again represented by Mohammad Alimuddin of Lilong accompanied by Mohammad Ashraf Ali from Irilbung, Yairipok and Muhammad Chaoba Mia from Charangpat Khongjom. The population of Muslims in 1961 had increased 48,588. So Muslim representation kept pace with the increase in population.

In the second Manipur Territorial Assembly, 1967 – 1969, there were two Muslim members in a house of thirty four viz. Mohammad Alimuddin and Mohammad Ashraf Ali of Irilbung, Yairipok Top Chingtha. Mohammad Alimuddin maintained his position as a good representative of the Pangals in Manipur. With the enactment of the North Eastern Areas (Reorganisation) Act 1971 by the Indian Parliament, Manipur was conferred Full Statehood on 21st January, 1972, with a sixty member Legislative Assembly.

After Manipur attained statehood, in the first election to the Manipur Legislative Assembly 1972-73, in a house of sixty members there were five Muslim MLA's viz. Mohammda Alimuddin of Lilong, Mohammad Chaoba of Athokpam, Mohammad Habibur Rahman of Khekman, and Mohammad Jalaluddin of Keirao. The population of Muslims at the time was 70,969. What is striking about this election was the election of Muslim from a minority community, as the First Chief Minister of Manipur State viz. Mohammad Alimuddin. Not only did he possess Charisma, but he commamded the loyalty and respect of the entire Muslim population and of Non-Muslims as well. This is apparent from his elevation to the highest post in government (Cabinet).

In the Second Manipur Legislative Assembly 1974-1979, there was a significant increase in Muslim Representation, the highest ever, seven members in all, viz. Mohammad Abdul Wahid from Kshetrigao, Mohammad Alimuddin from Lilong, Mohammad Ashraf Ali from Andro, Mohammad Chaoba from Wangkhem, Mohammad Habibur Rahman from Wabagai, Mohammad Jalaluddin from Keirao, and Mohammad Abdul Latif from Mayang Imphal. It is not possible to ascertain the reasons for this dramatic increase (the papers available in the Manipur Legislative Assembly commence from the year 2002 – earlier records were destroyed in a fire), but perhaps Mohammad Alimuddin's stature and popularity accounted at least partly for this increase. But Muslim representatives have always held one or more cabinet ranks since 1972 when the first election to the Assembly was held.

In the Third Manipur Legislative Assembly 1980-85, there was a decrease in the number of Muslim representatives. There were only three members elected: Mohammad Abdul Matalip of Keirao, Mohammad Abdul Salam of Wabagai, and Muhammad Muhamuddin of Kshetrigao. The Muslim population in 1981 stood at 99,327, representing 6.99% of Manipur's population.

In the Fourth Manipur Legislative Assembly 1985-1990, there were again three Muslim members-Mohammad Abdul Matalip, Mohammad Alauddin from Lilong and Mohammad Mohamuddin Shah. To the Fifth Manipur Legislative Assembly 1990-1995, was a New Muslim representative from Lilong, viz. Mohammad Hellaluddin Khan, also Mohammad Mohamuddin Shah from Kshetrigao. The population of Muslims had crossed on lac, and stood at 1, 33,535, registering a considerable increase.

In the Sixth Manipur Legislative Assembly 1995-2000, there was an increase in Muslim representation members four in all were Mohammad Abdul Salam from Wabagai, Mohammad Helaluddin Khan from Lilong, Mohammad Hessamudin of Moirang, and Mohammad Mahmuddin Shah of Kshetrigao. The last was elected in March 1998 through a by-election. The Seventh Manipur Legislative Assembly lasted only two years 2000-2001, and the Muslim members were reduced to one i.e. Mohammad Alauddin of Lilong. The Muslim population however continued to grow, in the 2001 census it was 1, 90,939 or 8.32% of Manipur's population.

There was an increased representation in the Eight Manipur Legislative Assembly, 2002-2007. Three Muslims were elected viz. Mohammad Abdul Salam from Wabagai, Mohammad Alauddin Khan from Keirao and Dr. Maniruddin Shah from Lilong. In March 2002, Mohammad Abdul Salam was made Minister of Cooperation, Minorities and OBC and Social Welfare in a Cabinet headed by Shri O. Ibobi Singh. By an order issued on 30th April, 2003, Mohammad Abdul Salam continued as Minister of Cooperation, Minorities and OBC, whereas Dr. Mohammad Maniruddin Sheikh was appointed Minister of State (Independent Charge of Fisheries) and Mohammad Alauddin Khan, Minister of State Public Health Engineering. Thus, all three Muslim elected MLA's held cabinet posts.

In the current Ninth Manipur Legislative Assembly there are two Muslim elected members viz. Mohammad Alaudin Khan of Keirao and Mohammad Helaluddin Khan of Lilong of these two, the First is Minister of RD and PR, MOBC and Fisheries.[33]

The representation of Muslims in government services continued after the merger of Manipur into the Union of India. Entry into the Combined Civil Services is on a competitive basis. The number of Muslims holding office in the prestigious Indian Administrative Service Manipur Cadre in 2009 stands at only three viz. Sohel Aktar, Commissioner Relief, Disaster, Management and Rural Development, A.R. Khan, Commissioner Labour, Md. Abdus Sattar, Commissioner Sericulture. One Muslim IAS officer is currently on deputation to the centre (Delhi).

In contrast to the paucity of Muslim IAS officers, there are a number of Muslims in the Police Service, both IPS and MPS (Manipur Police Service) Whereas some are serving as officers, a good number are serving as constables, continuing the tradition of Pangal Siphais in the Erstwhile kingdom of Manipur. There are also Muslims employed in the Government Sector, as Professors, lecturers, teachers, doctors, lawyers, engineers, technicians, also as Grade-IV employees.

Women's Role – Although Muslim women played no direct role in administration, governance and politics till very recently, there is no legal bar that prevents Muslim women from taking an active part in governance and politics. However, there is no reference to a Muslim woman administrator or government official either before 1891, or even between 1891 to 1947. This reluctance to enter into politics has changed as a result of the 73rd Amendment Act of 1992 of the Indian Constitution, which gives one-third reservation to women in the three tier system of local government.

This does not preclude women's participation in issues/events that affected the entire populace. During the Nupi-Lan or Women's uprising on 12th December 1939, Muslim women's participation is recorded. This women's uprising was a protest against the export of rice from Manipur, chiefly by the Marwari merchants residing in Imphal. The immediate cause of the outbreak was the great increase in the price of rice, following a poor harvest. The women demanded an immediate stop to the export of rice from Manipur. According to an account narrated by a correspondent of 'Mingshel', a monthly journal, (24th Dec. 1990), Meitei Pangal women who ran business as vendors in the market place, dealing in commodities like vegetables, eggs, tobacco, took part in the Nupi-Lal. In fact all the women vendors of

Khwairamband or Ima Keithel were asked to take part in an attack on a rice godown of a Marwari merchant Kasturi. In the melee that followed some women protestors were arrested. Among the Muslim women were included Shara Bibi, Shajaobi Bibi, Tombi Bibi, who were jailed. According to Shara Bibi herself, the Meitei Pangal women who joined the 1939 agitation were Yaima of Panggong, Apambi of Keikhu, Amubi, Noorjahan, Tombi, Amulala, Marem, Heiton, Hashi, Jamina, all of Khergao, Jamila of Sabal Leikai, Garam of Khergao, Dodi Achoubi of Porompat, Khambi (Rani mama) of Khetri Awang, Meherani of Khetri Mayai Leikai, Gulzan of Khetri Mayai Leikai, Leiren of Sabal Leikai, Thanil of Sabal Leikai, Tomba Bibi of Khergao, Shajaobi of Khetri Awang, Safarzan of Khetri Mayai Leikai, Kunjabi Bibi, Bodon Tombi and Sanabi Bibi.[34] This is a significant number, when we bear in mind that the total Muslim population of Manipur in 1951 was 37,197 (First Census) figures for earlier decades have not been recorded, but it must have been lesser, rather than more.

Other than this event, Muslim women's participation in political life is not recorded. In the Delhi Sultanate as also the Mughal Empire, Muslim women likeSultan Raziya, Gulbadan Begum, Salima Sultana, Maham Anagah, Nur Jahan, Mumtaz Mahal, Jahanara Begum, actively involved themselves in politics and administration/governance. But Muslim women in Manipur began to participate actively in the political sphere only when they were granted voting rights in 1948, to elect members to the First Manipur State Assembly 1948-49. Thereafter, they have participated in elections held in Manipur in the post merger period, but not as candidates aspiring for a seat. Their role was mainly passive, supporting the voting choice of the men folk in their family or leikai – they did not display and sign of free choice or independent thinking. As they played little or no role in decision – making. There are no Muslim women in the Administrative Service.[35] A few women however have acquired degrees and awards in the field of Education, Medical, Information Technology, Engineering, Law and can hold their own – they are however are a small minority. There is before them the inspiring example of the Prophet's wife, Bibi Ayesha, whose approval was sought by the people, when Hazrat Ali was appointed Caliph.

That women are slowly but surely, moving on the path of political empowerment, albeit at the grass root level, is illustrated by the election of Muslim women to Panchayati Raj institutions and to Municipalities. Some women hold the post of Pradhan, whereas others are elected members. They are thus acquiring a stake in power and privileges that have been traditionally the preserve of men.[36]

In addition, they are actively participating in the public arena, by taking an active role in developmental programmes relating to social welfare, public health (especially drug use and HIV), agriculture, co-operatives, and other related activities. They are now taking part in election campaigns, and canvassing and persuading female voters to go to polling stations to exercise their franchise. Their participation registered a marked increase in the recently held municipal and panchayat elections. Another momentous development is that a fairly large section of Muslim women voters are now making independent choices while casting their votes.[37] With compelling, persuasive examples before them like Hazrat Ayesha,Fatima Bin Qaib, Hazrat Jaiwara, the Manipuri Muslim women as they avail of greater and higher educational opportunities, as they grow in knowledge, proficiency, and technology, as they adopt a scientific temperament, will undoubtedly break the shackles that restrain them from realizing their full potential, come into their own in public life, and play an active role in politics. As there has always been Muslim representation in the legislature right from 1948, there is no reason why Muslim women candidates cannot just compete in Assembly elections, but also win decisively.

It is not that Muslim women have not been taking part in the public arena. Besides active participation in the Second Nupilal, Meitei Pangal women have formed many organizations at both the local and state level. Most organizations have social objectives but with political connotations e.g. the defence of human rights. Some prominent organizations are the Muslim Chanura Development Organisation with its head quarters at Hatta, Imphal East – this is the largest organization in Manipur. Most significant in the recent years with the growth of civic and political consciousness, Muslim women have mobilized themselves to air their grievances and demand fulfillment of their aspirations. They act as agents of social and political change.The Kangleipak Muslim Chanura Marup was the First Muslim Women's organization. It was formed in 2003 to lend support, and participate in the state women's movement. The women had played an active role in the communal riot (Meitei – Pangal) that occurred in 1993, which was brought to a close in a very short span of time. (38) Other local organizations and Meira Paibis (torch-bearers), among the Meitei – Pangal women, participated in the peace rally organized by Apunba Manipur Kanba Lup, All Manipur Club Organisation and the National Identity Protection Committee on 20th September 2000. Their participation reveals a heightened degree of political awareness, as they are cognizant of the fact that development takes a back seat when peace is absent.

Another instance of political consciousness is their participation in the demand for preservation of the territorial integrity of Manipur. They play an important role in instances of illegal detention, arrest of innocent persons in the state.

Drug use and drug-trafficking have political ramifications, and Meitei-Pangal women have joined the state movement, as also that of civil organizations like AMADA (All Manipur Anti-Drug Association) and CADA (Committee on Anti-drug and Alcohol), to stop the proliferation of drug use and drug-trafficking, and to counsel and rehabilitate drug users. Through their activities they play the role of watchdog to society (Manipur is situated in close proximity to the Golden Triangle). Another pro-active Muslim women's organization is the Ushoipokpi Tharourok Women Development Association, Ushoipokpi, Lilong, established in 2000.[39]

Many Muslim women are members of women's umbrella organizations of the state, besides the network of Meira Paibis in Muslim villages, who act as pressure group. These women have slowly but surely begun analyzing and questioning customs and traditions that tend to marginalize them.(40) As Muslim women share great commonalities with Meitei women, they come together on a joint platform, to demand their rights and seek redress of their grievances.

References

1. A. Hakim Shah Khullakpam, op.cit., pp. 33, 35.
2. Ibid., pp. 50-51.
3. Faroque Ahmed- Multidimensionality of Ethnicity in Manipur –From Conceptions to Substantivity, with special reference to Muslim Ethno-historical Evolution, p. 9.
4. Gangmumei Kabui, op.cit., pp. 217-218.
5. Faroque Ahmed, op.cit., p. 9.
6. Thangjam Subhas Singh, op.cit. p. 137 cit. L. Ibungohal and N. Khellachandra Singh (Ed) Cheitharol Kumbaba Imphal 1989, p. 33, And B. Kullachandra and Badaruddin op.cit., p. 2.
7. Ibid., p.136 cit N Basanti Devi 'A study of political History of Manipur from Pakhangba to Khagemba –Unpublished Ph.D Thesis MANIPUR University, 1988, p. 214.
8. Ibid., p. 139 cit,O. Bhogeshor and Janab Khan op. cit., p. 33.
9. Ibid., p.140 cit. Kh.Chandra Sekhar (Ed.) op.cit., p. 36.

10. Ibid., p.141.

11. A. Hakim Shah Khallakpam op.cit., p. 5.

12. Ibid., p. 61.

13. Ibid., pp. 74-101.

14. Thangjam Subhas Singh-op.cit., p.145 cit. B. Kullachandra and Badarudin.

15. Ibid., p.146 cit Kheirudin Khullakpam, pp. 40-41.

16. Ibid cit B. Kullachandra and Badaruddin, op cit., p. 94.

17. A. Hakim Shah Khullakpam, op.cit., pp.101-103.

18. Thangjam Subhas Singh, p.147 cit. B. Kullachandra and Badaruddin, pp. 90-91.

19. Ibid., p. 105.

20. Collection of Study Circle Sub-committee under Prof. Riyazuddin Choudhury-All the above participated in the Anglo-Manipuri War 1891- corroborated by M. A. Janab Khan Ipham in '1891 Gilanda Yaoruba Manipuri Muslim Lalmishing', published in Mingshel Vol. 38-40, Imphal October 1993, pp. 41-44.

21. A.Hakim Shah Khullakpam op.cit., pp.107-110.

22. Thangjam Subhas Singh, op.cit., p.149-152 cit. Meitei Pangal Hourakpham, Appendix, p.1.

23. A. Hakim Shah Khullakpham, op.cit., pp.113, 117, 120.

24. Thangjam Subhas Singh, op.cit., p.142.cit.Kheiruddin Khullakpam- Turko AfghanChada Naoda, Lilong, 1997, p. 54.

25. Ibid., pp.142-144.

26. A. Hakim Shah Khullakpam, op.cit., pp.122-126.

27. Ibid., pp.75-137.

28. Ibid., pp.188-189.

29. Ibid.

30. Ibid., pp. 204-219.

31. Ibid., pp.187-246.

32. Ibid., pp. 65-273.

33. SOURCE-Manipur Legislative Assembly.

34. A. Hakim Shah Khullakpam op.cit, pp. 259-260.

35. Laljan Begum-Muslim Women's Educational Status in Manipur, p. 4.

36. Syed Ahmad Status of Muslim Women in Manipur, p. 59, op.cit

37. Ibid.

38. Ibid-Women Empowerment and Development-A case study of Manipuri Muslim Women, p.79.

39. Tingneichong Gangte, op.cit., p.79.

40. Syed Ahmed op.cit , p.17.

Conclusion

The Muslims came to Manipur from 1606 onwards, although a small number may have entered prior to this date. What was significant about their migration was the fact that once settled in Manipur, they made it their home. They never returned to their original homelands, they married Meitei women, adopted Meiteilon as their language, and assimilated the culture of Manipur to such an extent, that they came to be known as 'Meitei – Pangals' Meitei' after the dominant Meitei community in the Imphal valley. They were treated well by the Manipuri kings and given suitable employment. Because of these factors, there was a gradual increase in the population of Muslims in Manipur, with the exception of the period of the seven years Devastation of Manipur, when the Burmese carried away many Muslims as War captives. There was however a great increase in population from 1951 to 2001.

In social and cultural life, they amalgamated the traditions and customs of the local people, with the traditional practices and way of life of Muslims elsewhere, especially with reference to ceremonies surrounding the passage of rites. It was a harmonious blending, which enabled the Muslims to live in perfect accord with the dominant Hindu majority in the Manipur valley. The greater parts of Muslim Habitations are close to water bodies in the valley, because the fertile soil and abundance of natural resources enabled them, to adopt for their livelihood, agriculture or fishery as a profession. They also possessed skills in occupation like carpentry, soldiery, pot-making, poultry –farming etc and they are credited with introducing certain new technologies, as fór example, broadcasting of rice seeds and transplantation, as also the wheeling technique in manufacturing pots. The women augmented the family income through the maintenance of kitchen gardens and weaving. Many Muslims women work as vendors in the Ima Keithel, and others hawk their wares from place to place. Both men and women work as casual labour on a daily wage. Some women and girls are employed as domestic help.

Although the socio-economic conditions for a long span of time were by and large favourable to the Muslims, they were unable to derive maximum benefits, because they were impeded by a slow late start in education and an abysmally low literacy rate. Even when the Muslims realized the importance and necessity of education, they favored a religious oriented education and stayed away from secular learning. In fact, the first educated Muslims were Maulvis at the end of the nineteenth century. It was only after the end of colonial rule, i.e., in the seconds half of the twentieth century that greater progress of education of Muslims was evinced. Women were slower to make a start, and the figures for Muslim girls in Education, especially at the higher levels are negligible.

In the field of religion, greater emphasis was placed on the Quran and Hadith only in the twentieth century, although Manipuri Muslims right from the beginning professed Islam and were sincere in the profession of their faith. Currently more attention and emphasis is given to Islamic injunctions and a Haj committee was formed in 2003.

Muslims have always been employed in State service, even after the Merger of Manipur with India, their participation continues. However, Muslim Representation in the Administration, especially at the higher level is not satisfactory- On the other hand, they have always had a fairly good representation in the Manipur Legislative Assembly. Indeed, the First Chief Minister of Manipur State was a Muslim- Muhammad Alimuddin.

The position of women presents a kind of dichotomy. Most women work for a living, they are mobile, do not adopt purdah, and take active part in democratic movements on issues such as defending the territorial integrity of Manipur, protecting human rights and so on. But at home, although they make decisions relating to household management, and are Supreme in the kitchen, they play little or no role in decision-making. Simultaneously, they are quite vocal in the public arena. Some of them have been elected to the Panchayati Raj Institutions.

But Socio-Economic indexes today show that the Manipuri Muslims are behind, especially in the fields of Education, Science, Technology, Mass Communications, Health, Standard of living. Special incentives, measures and programmes are needed to enable the Muslims to come into their own, especially the women. Governmental and non-governmental Agencies have made a start, but much more needs to be done to empower the Muslim Community.

Index

Q

R